M000265971

"All of the stories shared by Acharya subtleties *that make me smile – and sometimes laugh – but always turn my focus inward, and allow a new perspective to open up. Each day, I remind myself of the gratitude I have for Acharya Shree; for his guidance which helps me to trust myself and see the world with clarity and understanding, and for his compassion and gentleness that inspire me to swim deeper into my sadhana, and further along my path. This is why I chose to dedicate my life to Acharya Shree's teachings; to begin walking closer to soul, and closer to true harmony and non-violence."*

- Miles O'Sullivan, Texas, USA

"Acharya Shree Yogeesh and his universal teachings have completely transformed my life. His teachings of non-violence, compassion, and love have immensely expanded those qualities within me. I have gained so much understanding about who I really am and what my true purpose is...this has become a realization of my soul. I once had a dream to live a healthy life, free like a bird, full of confidence and liberated from pain and suffering. I know that with Acharya Shree's guidance I am now on the real path that can take me closer and closer to this dream's existent reality. I continuously put love, dedication, time and effort into practicing Acharya Shree's teachings and techniques, which has given me unimaginable results. This has lead me to become an unimaginable, amazing, better me. I know that if anyone does the same and takes Acharya Shree's teachings to heart, they will become better people and will live a meaningful life full of satisfactions."

- Anubhuti, Texas, USA

To, Alexandra.

*Father is a Father, is a faith,
Mother is Mother is the truth.
Think about it and be on Path.*

Peace and Love

Secrets
of
Enlightenment

Volume I

Acharya Shree Yogeesh

Siddha Sangh Publications

SIDDHA SANGH PUBLICATIONS
9985 E. Hwy 56
Windom, Texas 75492
info@siddhayatan.org

Copyright © 2004 by Acharya Shree Yogeesh
Cover design: Rob Secades

All rights reserved. No part of this book may be reproduced or transmitted in any form, without written permission from the publisher, except by a reviewer, who may quote brief passages in a review; nor may any part of this book be reproduced, stored in a retrievable system, or transmitted in any form or by any means electronic, mechanical, photocopying, recording, or other, without written permission of the publisher.

ISBN - 0-9843854-1-X
ISBN - 978-0-9843854-1-6

LCCN - 2013942019

Printed in the United States of America.

Disclaimer

Please note that not all exercises, diet plans, or other suggestions, mentioned in this book are suitable for everyone. This book is not intended to replace the need for consultation with medical doctors and other professionals. Before changing any diet, exercise routine, or any other plans discussed in this book, seek appropriate professional medical advice to ensure it is acceptable for you. The author and publisher are not responsible for any problems arising from the use or misuse of the information provided in this book.

TABLE OF CONTENTS

INTRODUCTION

The word "spirituality" can be defined in so many ways. When you browse through the 'spirituality' section of a bookstore, you'll find topics such as astrology, tarot, law of attraction, angels, religion, and general self-improvement. We often turn to books because we are seeking an answer to something we feel within ourselves; maybe we are curious about a topic; maybe we are trying to overcome doubts. Or, perhaps we are seeking truth.

Being an enthusiastic book-reader when I first began my spiritual path at 17, I became immersed in many seemingly spiritual books, ranging from Wayne Dyer, Eckhart Tolle, Louise Hay and Deepak Chopra. I was seeking the truth. Sadly, though the books from these authors were quite inspirational, many concepts felt both temporary and contradictory. I wanted more. I didn't want theories or philosophies, scriptural commentaries, or interpretations; I wanted truth - I wanted wisdom. I wanted permanent, unwavering, total transformation. I wanted to learn from someone who taught and spoke from their own enlightenment and actual experience of soul.

Fortunately, I didn't have to wait long, and met my guru, Acharya Shree Yogeesh, when I was just 20-years-old. Over the course of nearly a decade, Acharya Shree has helped me break away from ideologies that prevented me from knowing truth, taught me to be steady and patient, understand and transcend the violent experiences I went through in Iraq, and dissolve clouds of confusion, giving me clarity. Not only did I awaken my soul, but with his guidance I've experienced my own realizations.

If a master is genuine, they won't be looking for followers; they look for those students that have the potential to become masters themselves - always remember this during your search. Knowledge comes from the outside; realization comes from within. Acharya Shree wants you to experience your own realizations, in order to lift your soul higher and become a master.

The book you now hold in your hands contains many gems - gems which can create incredible changes in your life if you practice them with your whole heart. It's important to remember that you cannot just read this book and expect change. You have to understand it deeply, read it again and again, and then practice what you have learned. While you read this book, you might experience 'clicks', or, 'glimpses' - tastes of your soul. It's these moments that are helpful for your spiritual journey.

Secrets of Enlightenment, Vol I, is unlike any spiritual book that you've ever read; these lectures were transcribed and summarized directly from the words of an Enlightened Master. In this era of flourishing technology, we have the capability to communicate with people in every nook and cranny of the world; whether they're in common meeting centers like cities, or out-of-the-way places, we can communicate with people that we may not have the means to meet in-person. Due to this technology – unlike in the past – we can record a master and listen to their words directly, rather than pass them by word-of-mouth through the generations, possibly losing the right concept. The best time for spirituality is now. Your time is now.

According to Acharya Shree Yogeesh, spirituality is the path and process of dissolving karma, awakening the soul, and lighting up the countless particles that belong to it. When your soul leaves the grip of karma, *completely* awakens, and all of soul's countless particles are lit, then you are in that state of highest consciousness – enlightenment.

Essentially, you have to make the effort to improve yourself, and slowly dissolve your karma.

Soul is shapeless, formless, body-less and is infinite knowing and power. Its nature is total bliss and ecstasy. Because the soul is in the grip of karma - like how the clouds block the sun from shining through - it suffers. You suffer.

KARMA BASICS

Karma is a universal law, which states that you collect karmic particles based on your intention combined with your actions - whether mental, emotional, physical, or by speech. It's a common saying, "Do good, get good karma. Do bad, get bad karma," but karma is often misunderstood. There is a depth to karma that many are not aware of. The science and details, such as how the soul collects karmic particles, the workings of the eight *ghatiya* and *aghatiya* categories of karma, what practices can be used to dissolve specific karmas, and the states of consciousness that the soul rises through towards enlightenment and liberation, are some examples of the intricacies of karma that only a master can help you to understand.

In each moment, whether sleeping or awake, karma is being accumulated as a result of open holes - spiritual ignorance - where karmic particles pour in and mix together with your soul. For example, if you have not conquered your anger 100%, anger will continue to be a source for you to collect karma. Or, if you have not dissolved your jealousy 100%, you will be able to collect karma when you are jealous. It is easy to dismiss the possibility of having these karmas if you don't experience something negative like anger, but the particles that disturb the soul are subtle, so it is difficult to know when they are active on the surface. Often times, these subtleties come from karma collected in previous lives, therefore you may not be aware of how they are affecting your spirituality in this life. Unless you work on yourself and practice awareness, you will always collect karma. The more karma you collect, the less opportunities the soul has to awaken itself and break through the clouds.

It is because of karma that the cycle of birth and death continues. When the time comes - after much effort and deep understanding - the soul will be free, realize its enlightenment, and become liberated from the cycle at the end of that life.

To be free, we need to stop collecting new karma by closing the open sources (like plugging the in-flow of water into a reservoir), then dispose of the karma we've already collected throughout our countless lifetimes (draining what's left within the reservoir). Even if you dissolve just a tiny bit of karma, it is a great weight lifted off of your soul.

Karma can be broken down into eight categories. Four are called *ghatiya*, which are the karmas that obstruct the soul from knowing itself. The other four are called *aghatiya*, which are about the body where the soul dwells: how long the body can survive *(ayu karma)*; the type of body like bacteria, insect, animal or human body *(nam karma)*; societal status, such as being born in a poor or wealthy family *(gotra karma)*; and lastly, the mental,

4

emotional and physical pain and suffering experienced *(vedaniya karma)*. Because you are on the spiritual path, it is very important to understand the karma categories and the ways that they block your soul.

THE FOUR GHATIYA CATEGORIES

Jñānāvaraṇīya Karma. These karmas obscure the soul from its own knowledge.

- *Mati-Jñānāvaraṇīya Karma* blocks the knowledge transmitted to the senses (ie. When you read something and forget what you have read, or if you put your hand in boiling water and you feel it is cold.)

- *Sruta-Jñānāvaraṇīya Karma* blocks the knowledge acquired by interpretation (ie. When you are listening to a teacher, the concept is not easily grasped, or you fall asleep or misinterpret words, symbols, and gestures.)

- *Avadhi-Jñānāvaraṇīya Karma* blocks knowledge in a limited way (ie. Your inner-vision is blocked from experiencing or describing objects up to a certain distance from where you are located.)

- *Manah-Jñānāvaraṇīya Karma* blocks you from seeing mind-particles (ie. You cannot see if your mind or another's mind is playing games or tricks on you.)

- *Kevala-Jñānāvaraṇīya Karma* blocks absolute knowing of the soul (ie. When you are on the wrong path, or not seeking spirituality, you are unable to have soul-knowing.)

Darśanāvaraṇīya Karma. These karmas block the soul from having right vision, or seeing things as they really are.

- *Chaksur-Darśanāvaraṇīya Karma* blocks visual perception (ie. You cannot see with your eyes, be born blind, color-blind, etc.)
- *Achaksur-Darśanāvaraṇīya Karma* blocks all the other senses, except your eyes (ie. You are not able to hear, smell, taste, feel, etc.)
- *Avadhi-Darśanāvaraṇīya Karma* creates limited vision (ie. A person might express their spirituality using unfamiliar language and you immediately judge and dismiss them as non-spiritual. You are not seeing them as they really are - spiritual, but disguised.)
- *Kevala-Darśanāvaraṇīya Karma* blocks your clear vision of the soul (ie. You do not have any glimpses from the soul or cannot see through to the soul.)

Mohanīya Karma. These karmas create delusion around the soul about what is truth and how to act. It is considered the most dangerous and most difficult to dissolve, because these are the largest and easiest holes to fall through that will bring you a lot of karma.

- *Darśana-Mohanīya Karma* hinders understanding of spirituality and truth.
- *Mithyātva-Karma* causes beliefs in false teachings and false gurus and prophets (ie. A person gets trapped into fake spiritual teachings and sees false gurus as saints.)
- *Cāritra-Mohanīya Karma* disturbs right conduct and is mostly produced by the four passions *(kshāyas)*: anger *(krodha)*; ego *(māna)*; deceitfulness *(māyā)*; greed *(lobha)*. Karma is also collected through six non-passions *(nokshāyas)*: evil laughing *(hāsaya)*, liking *(rati)*, disliking *(arati)*, sorrow *(śoka)*,

fear *(bhaya)*, and disgust *(jugupsā)*. In addition, karma is collected in desiring and lusting for sexual pleasures *(vedas)* with a man, woman or hermaphrodite - this excludes expressing love.

Antarāya Karma. These karmas block the soul from enjoyment and achievement.

◆ *Dāna-Antarāya Karma* prevents you from achieving any kind of success. It is collected when you block a person from helping another (ie. When you convince someone not to donate to a charity that they are passionate about, then you collect Dāna-Antarāya Karma. As a result of collecting this type of karma, when the time comes that you want to do good and/or achieve any kind of success, something prevents it from happening, and you cry over it and wonder, "Why?")

◆ *Lābha-Antarāya Karma* blocks any benefits that could be received throughout your life. (ie. You distract someone from achieving their goals, so when you should receive the benefit of something good, it is blocked.)

◆ *Vīrya-Antarāya Karma* blocks the soul's will power and physical/mental strength. (ie. You make a person weak, hurt their self-esteem, or prevent someone from taking the spiritual path, so as a result, you will not have any will-power to achieve your own goals - societal or spiritual.)

The science of karmic law is vast. The aforementioned is just a brief summary. I mention all of this because it is important to understand why things have happened to you and why you have ups and downs on the spiritual path. Unless you understand karma and its different types, it will be difficult to progress. Often times we blame God, curse others, and are upset when things in life do not go our way. The best thing to do, Acharya Shree says, is to take responsibility and put efforts to awaken your soul.

In order to ignite the soul and begin dissolving karma, you need to create a spark.

FIVE GEMS FOR ENLIGHTENMENT

Non-violence. First and foremost, you must learn to practice non-violence in your life. Non-violence *(ahimsa)* is when you are in oneness with all living beings. Acharya Shree always says, "View the world as your family. If you knew all livings beings are your family, you would not hurt or kill them."

The way to begin practicing non-violence is to be vegetarian. Being vegetarian is a requirement for enlightenment. Eat fruits, vegetables, grains and beans. Mother Earth provides so much vegetation, there is no need to kill animals to fill your stomach. Killing animals is a form a violence and accumulates a lot of karma. When you eat meat, poultry and seafood, you are supporting the industry which perpetuates the supply and demand cycle - more deaths to animals, and more karma to block your soul.

Have you ever seen what happens at the slaughter houses or chicken farms? The animals experience a lot of pain, live in fear and experience great terror at the moment of their death. That fear, adrenaline and negativity enters their blood when they are being murdered. Remember, you are what you eat - their fears, anger, stress and anxiety enter your blood. Practice non-violence by being vegetarian, and not only will you save many lives each and every year, you will also not collect karma.

Also, practice non-violence in your communication, thoughts and actions. Start breaking your habit of using bad words. They are unnecessary and they can be hurtful. Watch the words you use. Don't scream or yell. Speak nicely. Be aware of the thoughts you have. Be away from negative thinking or violent thoughts. If you begin to think negatively or violently, change your thinking immediately to something positive or begin reciting divine sounds *(mantras)*. Be non-violent in your actions. Be watchful where you are walking as to not hurt any living being. Don't crush spiders or ants, instead bring them outside. It is not their fault they are lost. Put into practice any preventative methods that will keep bugs out of your home. If you leave food out and you attract ants, you will collect karma for being careless and now having to kill hundreds of ants. Remember, you are ultimately responsible.

As the 24th Tirthankar Mahavira once said, "Let live and live."

Discipline. Discipline is what helps you advance on the spiritual path. By doing your spiritual practices, whether its *dhyan* (meditation), *japa* (mantras), *pranayama* (breathing), etc., you will begin to burn the toxins in your blood, bring clarity to your mind, and remove any spiritual, mental, emotional or physical blockages. Unless you do it, you won't receive the benefits. You can read many "how-to" books, but it won't matter since you didn't put any of the "how-to's" into practice. You can read how to plant a flower in the garden, but it doesn't count unless you go to the garden and plant the flower. Discipline helps you conquer any laziness, which is also a type of karma. Discipline keeps you on track.

Discipline shows you are willing to put efforts even on those days when it would feel better to wake up later or go to bed sooner. Discipline means action. Action, even a little step, takes you further along the path. Don't expect enlightenment without putting efforts.

Tapas. Tapas are forms of spiritual practices that are meant to create fire within the body. It is the fire that helps burn the toxins, karma and prevent diseases. Some forms of tapas are water-fasting, dry-fasting (no water), and pranayama. In general, it is safe to water-fast or dry-fast for a 24 hour period - always consult your doctor before starting any kind of fast.

Friendship. Be friends with all living beings. If you are in friendship with all living beings, you will not hurt, harm or kill them. You will be an honest, trustworthy, loving and kind person. You are already good to those you love, but don't limit your love to just family and friends. Embrace all living beings. Send them your love, peace and joy.

Compassion. Compassion is a form of non-violence. It is a concern for or feeling sympathetic for the pain and suffering experienced by any or all living beings. When you are compassionate you are kind to others, or help them in some way to alleviate the pain and suffering they might be experiencing. Sometimes it is your smile that helps a random stranger who is feeling down. Sometimes it's belonging to an activist group that fights for animal rights or volunteering at a children's shelter to give them inspiration and to remind them they are loved. Compassion is forgiveness. Compassion is rescuing a spider from your home and placing it outside, instead of killing it. Compassion can be listening to someone that has gone through a traumatic experience, and even if you don't have anything to say, you were there for them. Compassion is activating your heart's love and desire to help. When you are compassionate, you love all living beings... and all living beings love you.

The Five Gems for Enlightenment are some of the helpful treasures I found within Acharya Shree Yogeesh's book. I'm sure you will discover your own.

You have the potential to be enlightened. It requires hard work to dissolve your karma. Anything worth fighting for is always worth it in the end. You are fighting to live by, and know the REAL YOU. Enlightenment is the same way. Put efforts on your spiritual path. Never give up. When life throws storms at you, do your best to be balanced and ride out the waves. Be non-violent. Be disciplined. Be friendly. Be compassionate. Love all living beings unconditionally. Put efforts and you will grow.

May you find the gems within *Secrets of Enlightenment, Vol. I* to totally transform your life.

Believe in yourself.

Love yourself.

Know yourself - because hope for a better world starts with you.

Sadhvi Siddhali Shree
Chief Disciple of Acharya Shree Yogeesh
Spiritual Director of Siddhayatan Tirth

TURYAM

This New Year is a very special year. 2002 added up is four, and four is considered to be a very beneficial number, making the year we have just entered an extremely special year. The number four, whose symbol is the square, has a special meaning. It represents the fourth dimension, which in Sanskrit is called *Turyam*.

Scientists, familiar with the three dimensions of width, height and length refuse to acknowledge this Turyam or fourth dimension. In their skepticism they haven't put forth any scientific evidence on this matter. No scientist has ever been able to realize the fourth dimension as of yet. In fact, they have chosen to remain unaware on the fact that only Turyam, or the fourth dimension, is the dimension that gels the whole of life into one. Apart from a few mystics who are eager to understand the science of the soul and are willing to experiment on it, no one else has even attempted to understand it. And hardly anyone knows that without it things remain incomplete. However, this dimension is very difficult to achieve. Because it cannot be scientifically proven, very few are willing to tap into it or are willing to take that step which is beyond comprehension.

Turyam can be perceived only in that space where there is no length, no width and no height. Actually, it is immeasurable. This is why it is very difficult for our finite mind to grasp it. Unless mind goes beyond itself, directly into the experience of total relaxation, it will be impossible to realize the fourth dimension. Turyam is the inner and outer space, it is the emptiness, and if you can live in this dimension you will be living in that space in which soul is realized. In spite of this, the majority of people live their lives unaware of even the third dimension. Their lives are totally linear. What does that tell you about human beings and their aspirations? People would have much more clarity if they understood the third dimension. Can you imagine how much further they would be if they could live in the fourth dimension?

For centuries, different societies have created situations for space to be experienced, but now, in our modern times, these situations have lost their true meanings. Why do you think holidays have been fashioned? Exactly to create the deep state of relaxation needed to discover what is beyond the known. It is through relaxation that the possibility is heightened and emptiness is experienced. This is why in India instead of the word "holiday" we use the word *avakash*, which means emptiness, or where newness can come in. But if there is no place and no space, no things can come in. So find the place and the space where something of real value can enter you. The word avakash tells you to find the emptiness.

Once in India, a monk gave a lecture. In front of him he had a glass of water filled to the rim. He took the glass, and he used it as an example to show the audience it was impossible to drop anything else into it. The teacher took a leaf of *tulsi* (basil) and he placed it in the glass of water, and the water did not overflow. The teacher, with his example, emphasized the fact that even though things seem complete, space could still be found in them.

This is why in Hindi we do not say "holiday" or "vacation"; we say avakash, which means the space for emptiness in which the fourth dimension happens. But you are overloaded with thoughts and ideas. This is why you have no space available for anything else to enter. As a result, avakash, or the fourth dimension, becomes impossible. So holidays, vacations or avakash came into being exactly for this purpose, to create that atmosphere in which relaxation can happen. Madame Curie, the moment she was able to let go completely and dissolve all of her tensions, went into a deep sleep, and the formula she had searched to discover for so long came into her being during her sleep. Once she let go fully she became completely relaxed. It was in that deep relaxed state that she achieved her goal.

It is in relaxation that space/emptiness happens and that the fourth dimension can be experienced or realized. When you are fully relaxed the possibility is present for Turyam, the fourth dimension, to descend into your soul.

So have avakash, have the space. As yet, you are filled with so many ideas and so many thoughts just like the glass of water I just described to you. You have no space available for the fourth dimension to happen. When all the ideas, mind, and thoughts are fully dissolved you will realize that suddenly space is created. This is why this year has meaning, and it will be a very special year in many ways. Then Turyam, the fourth dimension, has a greater possibility to enter the heart of the whole world. Who knows: maybe all of these countries will change their ideas and the outcome of this change will be world peace.

When space is created the world will be much more relaxed. Tension has been building up through the years and we have seen its results. Psychologically, before anything can become smooth, and before things can get better, they get fully tense. You have seen it happening worldwide. In this past year we have undergone lots of tension, but now that we have entered this New Year, things will smooth themselves out. This New Year will bring lots of great results and new ideas. You will see it. In reality it has already begun. Look at Europe; it is becoming united by one currency. Even some of the Arab countries are preparing to do the same.

So Turyam is the uniting force. However, this does not come easy. Just because you want it, it doesn't suddenly happen. It usually happens when tension reaches its climax. So in order to touch that point you must create that situation in which Turyam can touch you. Actually, Turyam, the fourth dimension, really means soul or light. You can touch it and embrace it, but with one condition: you must be able to completely let the tension go. Once tension is fully dissolved all the way from the bottom of your being, and from every cell of your body, you are automatically in that state. This is the reason why this year is a very significant year. The combination is four. Four represents soul, and soul means peace. I feel that all the countries are now thinking in this direction too. In fact, they are wondering how much longer can they go on fighting each other, or live in such tense environments filled with violence and killings. They have already begun to think in these terms and because of it, lots of peace might manifest. I really feel this is the year for peace.

So the number four, indicative of a square, and it is the main focus for the New Year. And unless there is a square there is no space, there is no avakash, in which all of your ideas, thoughts and mind have dissolved and you are fully into yourself. Only when you are fully into your being can you create the inner space. This is why this New Year has greater possibilities than previous years, especially when right guidance is with you.

The global tension we are experiencing might dissolve, and if somehow we are able to create this space and release ourselves from all the ideas which go on constantly in our minds, we will be exposed to the possibility for light to come through. We are experiencing the beginning of lots of changes, and know that a year like this year will not happen again until the year 2020, when the combination of the numbers will create once again the number four, or the square. In the meantime the process will continue on, and more peace will embrace the world.

THE REAL PURPOSE

If you were to ask me if there is a purpose for being here on Earth, my answer would be, "The fact that we are here is the most important and most beautiful purpose." We think that the sun is shining, the stars twinkle, and the moon is here because we are here. If we think that the sun is shining because of us or that the stars are twinkling because of us, we are absolutely wrong. All of these planets are here, have been here, and will be here no matter if we are here or not. They will go on shining without any purpose. It is we who think that they have purpose, but they don't.

But for you to be without a purpose is the most difficult phenomenon. You can only think in one direction, and this is why you need to have a purpose. You make a goal to get to a certain destination, but you don't know that the more goals you have, the more you lose yourself.

Why can't we find ourselves? Why don't we know who we are yet? Why are we not satisfied with just being here and getting to know our real selves? We don't appreciate it; this is why we are unable to accept this to be the most beautiful purpose of all.

Wanting to be the best doctor, the best engineer, the best artist or the best mother is not our real purpose even if we think it is. These purposes are only helpful for our survival because it takes money to survive in society. So we must work. However, along the way remember to spend time for self-discovery too. In life many things happen, but if you can accept everything without purpose, this will be the most wonderful thing you can do for yourself.

So think about your survival. In fact, go to school and get the right training, but be aware that if you solely depend on this aspect of life you will miss your real goal. Schools try to give people direction by teaching many subjects and by having the students learn everything. But this form of teaching could have a damaging result on the individual. Rather than helping the person to blossom, schools could destroy the person all the way to the core of his or her being. This type of teaching gives the student no freedom to explore and to find the area of his or her liking.

In India, Rabindranath Tagore was a Nobel Prize winner in the twentieth century. He was a great poet and in his autobiography he shared how much he hated school. But his parents wanted him to become somebody important, so they forced him to go to school. To skip school he would pour icy water in his shoes so he would catch pneumonia. He did this numerous times, and in all sorts of situations.

His real passion was not going to school. He wanted to be in nature all the time. Every time he was in nature, some unusual and extraordinary experience would consume his whole being, unleashing uncontrollable creativity. It was out of such extraordinary experiences that he began to write his first book of poems. Eventually, his genius talent was recognized and he was awarded the Nobel Prize. His great accomplishment, however, did not deter him from achieving his real goal. He was aware that writing this book of poems was not his real life's purpose. He accepted his creativity as a powerful expression of himself, and as the thing he loved most. He knew, however, deep in his conscious being, that being a poet was not his ultimate goal.

So, what do you really like? Would you like to be an artist? Would you like to be a doctor? Would you like to be a mother? What do you really want? You may or may not know what you like most. But if by chance you find a spiritual teacher who can encourage you to fully flow in the direction of your heart, eventually you might discover yourself. Remember, however, that any choice you make is never the real purpose of life. The real purpose is to know yourself. If you don't know yourself, how can you say that you are an artist? That you are a doctor? The first thing you have to know is yourself. But let me give you a word of warning: make sure you do not make this search your goal. Just be simple and find the way to flow and shine. Shine like a sun, like a star or like a moon – that's the goal.

I know that living in society prevents this shining. In society you need an occupation. After all, you want to be able to survive respectably and easily. You don't want to struggle, so you decide to become a doctor. But if this is not your heart-felt aspiration, the money that this brings you will not soften your struggle. This is why it is important that you find what you like the most. Don't make your choice merely because of money; make it because it is your inclination, and I assure you that your struggle in society will be lessened tremendously.

Maybe you have chosen to be an artist. In my experiences with artists, I've found that many of them do not want to survive in society as artists. They love to paint and to be able to create, so they choose not to make art their profession. Art for them is something that happens along the way. When it happens this way, then their creation will be a unique one, because when art comes from the heart it makes the person feel lots of happiness and love.

So, if you ask me what the real purpose of being here is, I'll say, "To know yourself, to grow spiritually and to shine." People are confused. They have mixed everything together. They think if they follow a certain ideology, a certain philosophy, or a certain religion, that they will be spiritual. They are wrong. Following any religion or following a certain school of thought does not make you spiritual. It simply makes you fall into a certain class, into a certain category, or into a certain group. You might know certain ideas and be able to discuss them with others, or you might have enough logic to debate others with because you've read lots of books and have acquired lots of knowledge. But that does not make you a spiritual person. You might be a religious person, but being religious automatically puts boundaries around you, thus putting you into a small box.

There are more than three hundred religions in the world today, maybe even more than five hundred. Every religion represents a small box. But spirituality is very vast. Even the word "spirituality" itself cannot contain spirituality. You must experience it to know its vastness. It has no limits and it makes a person extremely open in every way.

Experience life to its fullest. Then you will realize that the only purpose of your life is to know your true and most real Self. Peel away all the layers as you peel an onion. Peel until only nothingness remains. Awaken your inner guru and let yourself be. Be natural and welcome each experience that comes your way as a teacher who brings you the opportunity to know your real Self. Let life be your teacher and learn the technique of how to turn milk into butter. The real purpose of life is to be Self-realized.

LOVE

Love is a vast and vital concept, and God is in this love. Where there is no love, there is no God. Actually God only resides in love. This little word, love, is made of four letters. L stands for luck and life. O stands for ocean and openness. V stands for vitality and vastness. And E stands for eternity and energy. Vastness, openness, vitality and eternal energy, is God. In this wholeness everything is divine, and because you also exist in this you are divine too. The whole of nature including mountains, rivers, oceans, stars, moons and everything in it is divine. Love itself is divine. In the beginning it was love which inspired people to think of something beyond them, and this was when the concept of God was created.

If love happens, let it happen. It has been my experience that if you can develop this kind of love – and I am talking of supreme love – it must be shared. If you cannot find a person to whom you can give it to, if you cannot find a child to give it to, then give it to nature. Give it to the trees, give it to the mountains and rivers. And if this kind of love happens in you and you share it, you will get it back a hundred thousand-fold. Create this possibility. Be full of love and your love will become supreme love. When this happens all of a sudden you might dance, and you might sing without any meaning. Others might not understand your behavior and they might think you have gone crazy. Society will not understand. Society teaches that you can act, but not without meaning. Not only society teaches this, but economics follows in the same footsteps. Economics teaches us to collect, and to hold on to our collections. If you want to have money, you must collect it in the bank. This is what society and economics teach.

Contrary to society and economics, the spiritual world tells you to share. Bliss is in sharing. And this has been the teaching of every prophet. Consider Jesus at the last supper; there was only one piece of bread, which was shared among thirteen people. Sharing is the best thing that can happen to you. If you have anything and you share it, that sharing will become your bliss. And when you are full of this bliss, you will blossom like a flower without putting any meaning or reason into the sharing. The whole of nature blossoms without any meaning. Do birds chirp because of any meaning? No, they simply chirp. When the wind comes, trees and flowers all begin to dance without any meaning also. Look closely at nature, look at the sun rising in the morning and setting at night. Look at the butterflies or at the twinkling stars and you will see how natural all this is. It all happens naturally. Whether you ask for it or not, it will still happen.

This sharing is bliss, and I guarantee you that where there is sharing, bliss is there too. If you can develop to be as natural as nature is, you will obtain everything. Whatever you have, share it, even if it is knowledge. Share it: otherwise it will go bad. If you do not find a person to share it with, give it to nature. This is why Saint Francis of Assisi shared with nature. He couldn't find anyone to share his knowledge, his love, and his bliss with, so he went into the forest to share all he had with the animals and the trees. He even disrobed himself and shared his whole self with nature and he became full of light, full of love and bliss. As soon as you share anything it comes back to you a thousand-fold. So love is very powerful, and because of love people started thinking of God.

Economics teaches you to be a miser, society teaches you to be a miser, while the spiritual world teaches you to share and give freely. It teaches you not to hold on. In fact, the more you give the more divine you become. Whenever you give, you become higher, and whenever you take you become lower. This is a very natural law. Consider the ocean. The ocean is the lowest point on the Earth. Why? The ocean is never satisfied. It takes from thousands, even hundreds of thousands of rivers, and the ocean takes it all. On the other hand the cloud, which is high in the sky, always gives and gives. Whenever it is filled, it gives its rain to the Earth. So when you share you become like a cloud, and when you take you become like the ocean. This is just an example, but try to understand it. It does not mean that the ocean has no good qualities.

Love itself is a widening energy and if you can grasp it and share it, bliss will surely be yours. The sun gives its rays to the whole world. Just be as natural as nature is. Don't ever think that the sun rises and sets for you, or that the birds go on chirping for you. Maybe they are sharing and you are not even paying any attention. God is like a sun-ray, like birds chirping their tunes. It doesn't shout, "I am here!" It quietly, gently and peacefully penetrates you. But you need to open yourself to be penetrated. Your window needs to be open. If it is closed and the curtains are drawn, or if any other blockage is present, you will not benefit from those rays. So to be penetrated, you have to let go and be fully open. Whatever possessions you have, let them go. Open yourself and sharing becomes natural.

If you can do this, you will be a very special being. No matter what you are, no matter what abilities you have, share what you are. Do not compare yourself to others. You have to have the confidence. In fact, you have to be courageously crazy in order for God to penetrate you. If you are not crazy enough, I don't think God could penetrate you. But if God penetrates you, you will feel like a mother at conception. The mother feels fullness within her womb; she knows that something has changed. It will be the same when God penetrates you.

Love: such a simple word, but a most penetrating and powerful word. Understand it, live it fully, experience its power, and your Godhood will be realized one day. You can become a new moon on the horizon – loving, cooling and shining.

MIND

The spiritual journey consists of having to cross the darkness, which in simple language is translated as "mind." In English, mind is defined as one word, but in Jainism there are two words to describe it: *Dravya manas* and *Bhava manas*.

Dravya manas is that mind which is always busy everywhere. It is the marketplace inside you. It is always focused on outward things, but never looks inward. Bhava manas is the closest thing to the soul, but it is still mind. By purifying yourself and by understanding your ego, you will be very close to understanding who you are. You are one step away from suddenly jumping into your soul. This mind needs to be captured and trained, just like training a wild animal. If this training does not happen, it will be impossible to realize one's true identity of the soul.

Interestingly, your daily routine presents you with situations in which to realize the true identity of the soul all the time, but your lack of awareness prevents you from recognizing all the lessons you could draw from them. If only a little awareness could develop in you, those experiences could benefit you immensely, bringing you closer to realizing who you really are and what the soul is. You see many things, but you do not pay any attention to that which you are seeing and how powerful it is. You are not realizing your own power. Take your eyes, for example. Through your eyes you can see very far. Can you imagine if you could realize the power which works behind the eyes, and which gives you the opportunity to see? But you don't even bother to even think in these terms. You never even ask yourself what makes your two little eyes see so far or what powers them to see or where this power is coming from.

Have you ever thought about it? With such little eyes you can see so far. Their power travels so far. You can see stars, you can see planets, and you can see the moon. You really do not understand how extraordinary this is. You simply take everything for granted. You are underestimating yourself and you have no idea what it really is. You think that all that happens in your body is because of your brain, but where is the brain getting its power? All of your senses are functioning because of this power. Every sensation is felt because of this power and you think that this power is your brain. I'm sorry if I disappoint you by denying your belief. Your brain without this power will not function at all. It can be kept alive if there is oxygen, but to function is another story. The brain, just like your eyes, needs that power of the soul in order to function. It is the soul which gives power to your body, including the brain. And soul has infinite power. Discover it.

By traveling the spiritual path, you are coming back to realizing and knowing your infinite power. Pass through the dark and gain the courage and confidence to bypass your mind. It is in bypassing the mind that you will reconnect to your own supreme power or soul.

Without soul, your body will feel no sensations. Soul does not suffer: body suffers. However, body cannot suffer without soul power. It is its connection to the soul that makes the body feel suffering or joy. The soul is the only substance that has feelings, sensation and power; otherwise a body without soul is a body without life. A dead body has no power. It is because of the soul that the body has the power to feel, to see, to hear, to taste and to touch.

Walk in the dark, purge yourself and clear the way, and eventually you will come face to face with this light, with your power, with your soul. Understand and know that if soul is gone from your body, your power to think is also gone. But to realize the soul, you have to watch every action and activity that goes on inside and outside of you. Without soul you wouldn't be able to do anything. You couldn't feel, you couldn't sense, you couldn't enjoy or be happy, because without soul nothing functions. The combination is there, but the real thing, the life force, the *soul*, is missing. This is the reason why spiritual growth is so difficult. You must explore the depth within yourself until you come to realize the truth of what soul is. It takes courage, because to pass through the dark, especially the inner darkness, is frightening for everyone. No one wants to face his or her inner darkness. If you do face it, you can find out many things and you will gain the clarity, the light, to see the way. You will know all that is happening around you and you will be open to learn from everything. And everything you come in contact with will take you to your inner self if you are open to learn from the situation.

I remember an example: A very good person wanted to seek the soul, so he visited a saint, and the saint suggested one technique. "I can show you the path, but you must walk and follow my suggestions, and you will realize yourself," the saint said to the man. The man was really ready to listen and follow whatever the instructions were. The saint suggested for him to go to a cemetery and to shout and abuse every grave by yelling and saying all kinds of bad things without stopping until he had completed his task.

So the man left for the cemetery. At each grave he shouted and started using all kinds of profanity. "You are very bad, you are very cruel, you are not good, and you are this and you are that," he would yell. He continued until evening and then came back to the teacher. The teacher asked if he had found anything, but the man said no, he did not find anything. "Alright," the teacher replied. "Maybe tomorrow when you go back you might find something."

The next day came, but this time the teacher instructed him to praise everyone. Again the man went to the cemetery where he started praising everyone. "You were the best person; you did lots of good deeds while you were still alive. You were such a nice person, so gentle and kind," the man cried. The whole day he praised the dead until evening came, then again he came back to the teacher. The teacher asked him if he had found anything. "No," he said, "I did not find anything." Then the teacher became very angry at him, and he slapped him and pushed him and he told never to come back again. "I gave you a very easy technique to find the soul. Look at you! You came back again with nothing," the teacher said. The poor man did not know what to say. He did not understand what he was supposed to look for and he was really upset at the saint.

His first reaction was to think that maybe his teacher was not a good teacher. However, deep in his heart he knew he was a good teacher. So instead of going away, he bowed to the teacher and touched his feet and begged him to let him stay and said, "Please, please, I know that I am ignorant, but I want to know what reality is, what truth is, and what soul is." The teacher said, "I gave you the right technique and you did what I told you to do. You used profanity one day and you praised them on the next. Did you get any reactions? No, you didn't get any reactions. That's the way, that's the path. This is what I wanted to teach you."

Be like a dead person and have no reaction. No matter whether people praise you or abuse you, don't react or be bothered. If you are affected or if you react, it means you cannot search your soul. Non-reaction is the quality you need in order to search inside yourself.

Another good example to learn from is the mud. If you throw rocks into the mud, there is no reaction. The rocks simply sink. But if you throw a rock in running water, not only you will hear the sound, you will also see many ripples.

Where there is reaction, people will go on bothering you again and again. Learn from day-to-day life. Use your experiences to observe yourself and see your reactions. Every time you react, it means the person or the situation affected you. As long as you are affected, even if only a little, you won't be able to achieve enlightenment. Know that where there is reaction there is still lowness. In day-to-day life you can find many experiences which you can use to understand the soul. You can think about why you are reacting. If you can think through it, your reaction may dissolve or it might be brought to the surface. Two things can happen: you can think it over or you can let it surface, but I recommend you never to suppress it. Suppression is never good. You can think it over and ask yourself why you are reacting and what the result of this reaction will be. Will it hurt others, or will it hurt me? Think over the results, and if you understand why you react, then maybe, very slowly, all the reactions will be dissolved.

If you are still affected, then I suggest you get good guidance. And if you get good guidance you must be patient, because to really understand takes time and courage. If guidance is available, use it, but don't rush it. Simply listen and learn slowly. It takes time to really go beyond reactions. Understanding does not happen suddenly. Right understanding comes slowly, but once you have it, it is much easier to walk on the path. Even to walk in the dark becomes easier.

Why am I mentioning the dark, and why do I give it so much importance? Because darkness is eternal, and it is not artificial. All artificial things will crumble and will be destroyed one day. But all eternal things will always exist. Light is artificial and people like light. It means people love artificial things. This is why they become artificial. Nobody is born artificial. We are all natural at birth, but with time we have become unnatural. You can create artificiality, but it is not possible to create reality. Reality is always there. You can turn on the light, but you cannot turn on darkness. Darkness is eternal and it will remain eternal. When you turn off the light, darkness appears again. I suggest you have courage, patience, and most of all right guidance, and one day you will reach enlightenment. Understand your mind and the darkness of ignorance will dissolve by itself.

INNOCENCE

Innocence is the key to entering the Kingdom of God, this is certain. But to be innocent is very difficult. Children are naturally innocent because they haven't yet developed their minds. They are born with the quality of innocence, which is very attractive to grown people. But as they begin to grow and accumulate more and more knowledge, they soon lose their innocence, and once innocence is lost, it is very hard to regain. You have to become a saint in order to regain your innocence. To regain your innocence, you have to enquire and learn about your mind and find the way in which mind can lose its power over you and no longer be in control of you.

You must first recognize that as you began to acquire knowledge, mind began to rob you of your innocence. And as your innocence was lost, mind took control of you. So to regain your innocence you must understand the process of how to liberate yourself from the grip of your mind. Once you understand the process and your mind is no longer controlling you, innocence begins to come back. And when this happens, each one of your actions will have innocence in them. Even if you were to be a king, or whatever else you may choose to be, if your mind is not in control you will be as innocent as a child. When you can become child-like, it means you have fully understood the mind's dynamics and how you were controlled by it.

The majority of people do not understand their mind, and thus cannot separate themselves from it. Mind and soul are like flowers in a prism. If you put some flowers near a white prism, the flowers will reflect into the prism. Now the flowers appear to be in the prism, when in reality they are outside of it. Mind and soul follow the same principle. They are two separate entities, but to you they seem to be one. So if you want to regain your innocence, you have to first fully understand mind's dynamics and realize that mind and soul are two separate things, not one. Unless you understand this, you will not know that you and mind are two separate things. If you can't realize this you will remain imprisoned in your mind, as the flowers are in the prism. And if this is the case, innocence will never be regained.

It was easy to be innocent when you were a child; mind, with all its ideology, had not developed yet. Nowadays things have changed; children can develop their minds within five years, and I would not be surprised at all if in the future children's minds developed even within a year. In this era of modern technology, ways of learning are so advanced. With so many electronic devices, our children will learn even more rapidly. Between television, computers and schools, even newborn children's minds can be developed in no time. However, their innocence also can be lost much quicker.

On the other hand, children's innocence is not so important. Their innocence will not help them to grow spiritually. To grow spiritually you need a new perspective, which is gained through experience. Children's innocence is devoid of experiences. Without experiences there is no realization, hence spiritual growth will be impossible.

Children and animals have the same kind of innocence. But in order to grow spiritually, this innocence has to be lost for mind to develop. Because animals cannot develop their minds as a human child can, animals therefore cannot grow spiritually. There are a few exceptions. It is extremely rare, but at times a child or an animal can grow spiritually even without a developed mind.

So, in order to grow spiritually the mind needs to be developed. Once developed, you need to let it go so that innocence can be regained. You need to go through and experience your mind until the day that you can see what mind is all about. When you can see that your mind is not you, it means that you have learned to look at your mind without colored glasses. You can see that the flowers are not in the prism, but outside of it. Now your innocence will be very helpful to you. Without developing your mind, you would have remained innocent, but this kind of innocence will not be helpful to you at all; it would make it impossible for you to live in society. This is not the kind of innocence I suggest for you to achieve. The kind of innocence I am talking about is totally different and does not belong to this category. First of all, you have to learn a lot - as much as you can. Read hundreds of books, or listen to as many lectures as you can. Listen to them carefully. Even though sometimes you are serious about listening and at other times you are not, somehow knowledge is still entering and penetrating your being. Also, by accumulating more knowledge, your mind will be developed even more. That's why I suggest to people that to be intelligent is not a curse. By intelligence I don't mean that one person is better than another because one can read faster than another, or because one person understands history better than another. One person cannot possibly be intelligent in every field.

We are all born intelligent, but we have to figure out which fields our intelligence flourishes and excels in most easily. Sometimes it is difficult to determine which fields we have an aptitude for, but with the right guidance they can be discovered. Schools can help children to find their way, but they might not necessarily guide the children towards their real interests. Maybe the child has been forced to learn certain things which were not really in the child's best interests, things that consequently destroy the child's innocence to the point he or she can never regain it. That's why sometimes a guru is needed in order for people to recognize in which direction their intelligence works.

A child's innocence seems to be the purest type of innocence, but it is not. True innocence is developed only after you have first collected all kinds of garbage. Without going through all this garbage, pure innocence cannot be developed. If you remain innocent like a child, this innocence could be abused. You would be taken for granted, since the other side of the coin has not been experienced yet. In fact, you wouldn't even know you are innocent. It is only after much collecting that real innocence can stick and can take root in you.

Go on and collect all kinds of information, and one day, when you learn to bypass the mind, when you learn to bypass the body, and when you learn to bypass the thoughts, real innocence will be regained, and this innocence will lead you back to the source. This is pure innocence. This innocence takes you very far. There you will discover all that which was not possible to discover previously: the true meaning of life. When this innocence is regained, the Kingdom of God is achieved. However, to achieve this innocence is very difficult. But if curiosity compels you to discover truth, nothing will hold you back, no matter how difficult it is; you will regain what was always yours to begin with: the true innocence, the natural one, which leads you towards enlightenment.

ULTIMATE EXPERIENCE OF LOVE

The word love has many meanings, but few people are aware of what this wonderful word really means. When love speaks, it fills us with life, affecting everyone who hears it. If you were very sad, unhappy or worried, and someone came near you and said, "You are so lovely, you are so loving, you really are a very loveable person," you would be amazed how quickly you would perk up. In an instant you would feel that all of your worries and tension had left you, as if something had really changed inside.

Love is a very unique phenomenon because it flows moment to moment; it does not flicker like many ideas do. Many words, many ideas, merely flicker. They give little glimpses and they soon disappear. In the past, love was considered to be like a flickering flame, but I cannot really support this statement. I cannot compare it to a flickering flame, and if I were to say that love is a flickering flame I would be very wrong. It is much more than that. Love is a light which shines everywhere at every moment. Love is like the sun. Love shines for everyone no matter what. The sun will rise and the sun will set, and if the birds sing or not sing the sun will not care. Whether the flowers bloom or whether the lotus opens its petals or not, the sun will not care. The sun will always rise, it will always set, and it will always shine. But don't think it shines for you. The sun will shine because that's the way the sun is: it is all about shining, and that will never change.

Love is like the sun; its shining has lots of power and its energy is very unique and life-giving. It can put prana, or life force, into a dead body. If a person has lost all hope and his life no longer has any meaning, or if he or she has lost caring and love for everyone, such a person has already faced death. However, imagine if in the next moment someone comes and says, "Oh, you are shining. You have a special radiance on your face. It seems that love is radiating all over you." Such loving gestures can suddenly, even if only momentarily, make the person regain his or her spark.

Love is the most wonderful phenomenon. Even the word itself is extraordinary. As we have seen in an earlier chapter, if you go a little further into it and you separate each letter you might have a taste of its infinite power.

"L" has the best meaning; it stands for "living being – or, life."

"O" stands for "ocean."

"V" stands for "vastness."

"E" stands for "eternity and ecstasy."

Love consists of merely four letters, but these four letters carry a lot of meaning, and very good ideas. However, if love is not sought out it can never be realized. The whole of life is hidden in it. Love is like a vast ocean full of ecstasy, full of living beings, and full of pranic energy or life force. If everyone gets to know the real meaning of love, he or she will also know its infinite power. To know this is to know that every living being, including you, is here to experience and enjoy this vast and infinite ocean. That's the reason Jesus said, "God is love, and love is God." And this is the truth. Each human being has within himself or herself the seed of infinite power, and by following those four steps love can be realized. Once love is realized, your own infinite and supreme power will also be awakened.

Supreme power is God, and God shines everywhere. This power is always available. It is all around you and it can be felt. You can touch it; you can smell it in every moment and everywhere. This power has no boundary. You do not need to go to church or to the temple or to the synagogue to be with this power. In fact, it is because of boundaries that this power has been lost and that humans fight each other. You only know boundaries, not love.

Why don't people understand this beautiful word? On the surface, everyone says, "I love you, I love you so much." But this love is very different. A mother loves her baby, but she loves only her baby. She does not think to love other babies as her own baby. In this way, your love has boundaries. Love is like a vast ocean full of ecstasy, full of enjoyment and full of eternity. It tells many things and it is eternal. If you really want to feel alive, then learn the meaning of this beautiful word. Be open and you will enjoy supreme power. Supreme power is forever flowing. It flows everywhere and in many ways. It flows through birds' singing. What does it mean when birds are singing? It means that nature is happy. That is love. Love flows in the flowers when they are blooming. It means that they are happy, that they are enjoying life, and that they are in ecstasy. Nature does not make boundaries like we do. It is because of boundaries that we lose the real meaning of love, and therefore, the real meaning of life.

We say, "This is my house," but birds consider the whole sky to be theirs. Even birds suffer from boundaries. Know that where there are boundaries, there is no love. Where there is openness and vastness, there is no suffering. You need to be open to everything, not only to your family or to your parents, but also to every living being or non-living being. Nature is vast. This universe is vast. In fact, there are millions of galaxies. Do you think that this galaxy, this sun, is the only universe? There are millions of galaxies and million of suns and moons like these.

You should not be satisfied with any boundary. But what do you do? You make a little house and you are satisfied. Destroy them. Do away with all boundaries and be like Saint Francis of Assisi. He left all boundaries; he even threw away all of his clothes. He was a rich man's son, but once he came to realize that God is love and that God is not to be contained by boundaries, he chose to live his life without boundaries. God is a very, very big phenomenon.

In the animal kingdom, you don't find hate as you do among humans. I remember reading once that humans are the most dangerous animals in the world. Humans cannot really enjoy anything, no matter what it is. Humans only know how to have boundaries, and this is the real reason why enjoyment has disappeared from their lives. They are not open. I am not talking about being open-minded; many people already are. The openness I am talking about has nothing to do with mind. A person with an open mind can be considered to be nothing more than one looking out through a pinhole. Open-mindedness is still a narrow way of seeing reality. The openness I am talking about is totally different and it has nothing to do with the mind. The openness I am talking about flows through your heart and through your soul, and when it really flows you will experience real enjoyment. Otherwise your enjoinment has no meaning.

Try not to understand this openness through your mind. If you do, you will lose its real meaning, and the point will be missed totally. People suffer because of trying to understand it through the mind. If you are not told how much you are loved or how good you are, or if you are not told how loveable and charming you are, you feel absolutely dead and life has no meaning. My advice to you is never to consider love through the mind or you will miss the point. Feel it. Real love has no knowledge, only feelings.

You can feel the sun. There is no need for the sun to tell you anything. You can feel its warmth. The sun is felt through your eyes, through your skin, through your body, but not through your mind. If you insist on understanding through your mind, ask the people who live in Africa. They will tell you how much they hate the sun. They absolutely have no love for it. They think it is too hot. You can hear their thoughts saying, "Why is it shining only here and why is it giving so much heat?" But what you hear is their reaction, and thinking always instigates reaction. Because of mind, the people there do not want any sun. Remember, it is mind that makes you think like that. The sun will shine no matter what you say or do. But if you become aware only of shining and you don't get involved in any thinking, I assure you, the sun will not disturb you. Actually, for the first time you will learn to enjoy its rays no matter how hot they get. The sun has nothing to do with your reaction other than your expectation of how warm it should be. If you learn how to flow and protect yourself from the intense heat, your perspective might change. You might develop an awareness of its warmth, love and compassion.

If you take this attitude, you might discover many wonderful things in yourself. You might even surprise yourself and become inventive. Because of the sun's rays, many inventions are taking place every day. Artificial electricity has been created, power has been collected, and so much more. Why don't you come up with your own invention? But first you must learn how to feel. Stop your obsession with knowledge and your power to feel will develop. Through knowledge you cannot learn to feel. Through knowledge you can only collect information, but you cannot have the experience of how to feel. And if you are not feeling, you won't be able understand the warmth, the compassion, or the shining the sun gives.

Love is like the sun. It shines, but to understand it you need to feel it fully through each pore of your being. Love can never be revealed if you cannot absorb it so fully. Love is not the language of the mind; it is the language of the body. Your body speaks to you all the time, but you do not understand its language; and when your body speaks it means that love is flowing. But don't confuse it with the language of falling in love. That is merely attraction. Or with the fact that you love your child. That love is the language of the mind. I am talking about something different, and it happens when every cell of your body feels love for the whole cosmos, with every living and non-living being, and not merely with the parts. It happens when you are open and loving with the whole of life.

To understand this love is to bring life back to your body. When life flows through every cell of your body it means that love is flowing, and your body speaks. Everyone ought to go through the process of recognizing the language of love. This is the reason why I say that love speaks through your body. However, if love speaks through your mind it means it is no longer love, but is merely your idea of love.

Many people have very sensitive bodies and can perceive love's language very quickly. Understand that when I say that the body is sensitive, I am saying that the body has its own intelligence and language. Even animals or plants possess this ability. They do not have a language, yet they still communicate with one another. I have never heard them speak any language such as Hindi, German, Italian or Japanese. They feel each other and they care for each other. Human beings have lost this ability and have developed a very intricate form of communication instead.

We have created so many boundaries everywhere, unaware that where there are boundaries real enjoyment is gone. This is what is happening to humanity, and I predict that in the next half century people will really go crazy because they will become even more and more closed, and their boundaries will go on increasing. Remember: where there are boundaries, there is no love. There is no freedom for love to flow.

People are so rigid, they are so traditional, and every one of their emotions is bottled up so tightly. One day your emotions will explode if you don't gain the right understanding to feel the feelings of warmth towards everything, both living and non-living. If you don't feel connected and open to the whole, one day you will collapse. Openness is the best prayer you can ever recite. There is no other secret in prayer but a total openness of being. When you forget yourself and duality is gone, that's prayer. Either you remain or God remains. And when love flows inside of you, prayer automatically happens. Love is wholeness, and wholeness is the best prayer. I consider this wholeness to be God. Feel oneness with wholeness and all the boundaries will disappear automatically.

So praying to God means to create love inside, and to create love inside is to merge with that power and be one. It also means to lose your duality, forget yourself and surrender fully. To surrender means to forget yourself. If duality remains, it is bound to create disturbances. If you are used to being alone and another enters your space and stays with you, you will feel disturbed. Alone you are free. When you are alone in your room you can do whatever you want. You can frown, dance, shake your head. You can do anything – anything you want. You can even act like a crazy person. Nobody will disturb you or judge you. But as soon as someone is with you, you feel uneasy. That's why everyone feels uneasy with others.

Sartre, one of the great philosophers of the West, said, "Hell is other people." He never considered the hell Christians, Hindus, or Buddhists think of, but instead said, "Hell is other people." But where there is love, the "other" is gone. This means there is no separation, only oneness, and that this oneness is the link. It also means that there is no difference between you and the other. When two people are really in love, then they do not bother each other because they feel they are one. But if the state of oneness disappears it means that love is gone. It is this lack of love which separates us. It is inevitable that when love is gone, the other appears, and the other always disturbs.

To Sartre this is hell. Whenever you are bothered because of the other, you are already in hell. Hell is actually nothing but the absence of love. In those moments when you feel the other, or separation, or duality, it means that love is gone. You could be surrounded by thousands of people, but if you don't feel their presence or if you consider them as others, it means you have not learned the secret of love. Once your openness embraces the whole, love is automatically realized and other has dissolved.

When Jean-Paul Sartre stated that others are hell, he was referring to tangible things such as people, animal, birds, trees, etc. But now modern psychology is saying that the other is not only all of the above; it also includes all that which is inside of you, such as thoughts, ideology, your emotions of hatred or jealousy, and so on. Therefore, mental activities create tension. It is in this tension that the feeling of hell is experienced. Actually, unless the other is gone, you cannot taste heaven either.

You have to lose all inner and outer boundaries that you've created. Even those boundaries you create in your aloneness. When you are alone in your room, you are not really alone because the other is always there with you by your constant thinking you are with others. By thinking, you bring the person to you. By thinking, you are creating many people in your mind. Maybe you are in a little room away from everyone, but at the same time the whole marketplace is with you. Observe yourself and see how crowded you are inside. You think you are alone, but the reality is that you are never alone. You can do something about it, though. Remember that when the other is present, oneness is gone. To be with your being is to feel oneness, and once oneness happens, the other disappears. Know that as long as you go on clinging with your mind you will go on being attracted to the biggest marketplace, and in this marketplace it is impossible to experience love. Slowly get rid of all inner and outer boundaries and attachments and one day you will experience oneness.

Your first and most important lesson is to learn how to make the other disappear. By breaking away from boundaries you will learn the language of feelings. But as you are, your feelings still relate to mind and thinking. It is time you learn to forget yourself and merge with oneness. When you can truly feel no separation from anything, separation from any living being or non-living being, you are experiencing oneness. To know oneness is to know God. To know God is to know love. To know love is to be one with the whole universe, and that is the path towards enlightenment.

RELAXATION

We never keep our attention on being. We are forever busy enjoying things, which keeps us away from ourselves, and we go on living our lives unaware of what we are really doing.

Do you know what the most important thing we can do in this life is? It is to know ourselves. But we are so blind we can't even see how foolish we are. We think we are doing what helps us to know ourselves, when in fact we move further and further from the truth. We go to such great lengths to explore other galaxies, other planets, and we don't realize how foolish we are. We try to know everything, but in the process of doing so we miss the most important thing – ourselves.

Relaxation is the key from which we must start. To be relaxed you have to be centered within your being, because relaxation can only happen when the flow of energy is in the present, not when it is scattered all over. On the road of self-discovery you must be truly relaxed at each and every step. In fact, there isn't even a path to show you the way. The way has to be searched for by you, within you, not away from or outside of you.

In the beginning you may have to search many ways until you find what is most suitable for you. But to find it you must have patience. It takes time to find the right way. To become a doctor you don't study only a single subject, do you? There are many subjects to study before you can reach your sought-after destination and goal. You have to study many different things, even though many of the subjects are not even related to your goal. But by being exposed to so many different subjects, you might discover whether you are really interested in them or not. To follow anything wholeheartedly, you must be well suited for it. Thus, if it is not well matched for you, you might change your direction all together. The same approach or formula can be applied towards self-discovery.

Be open to really listen to the guidance you are receiving. However, don't listen through one ear and let it out the other. Retain and practice what you hear and try to apply what suits you most to your whole life. In the beginning, everyone needs guidance. To acquire right understanding is not an easy undertaking. Guidance is necessary. To simply understand is not enough. In fact, your lack of wisdom might lead you even further from reality. See, you don't only need guidance: you really need the right guidance. In order to acquire right understanding, the guidance has to lead you in that direction.

Right understanding is quite different from simply understanding. Look at yourself: you already have so much understanding, yet you are still not relaxed. Hopefully you are not here, listening to me, trying to acquire more knowledge from me too. I hope the reason you are listening is because you are seeking the right guidance. Don't be stuck in your knowledge: move further and discover yourself. Your soul has no limitations, and no boundaries. Soul flows everywhere, but with one condition: that you forget yourself and be relaxed. Otherwise you will miss the point completely.

Relaxation is a very important state of being. In this state, many things can flower in you, things which are otherwise missed if you are not truly relaxed. The cosmos is very generous. You don't have to go to it to receive. The cosmos comes to you. It descends through you in those moments when you are fully relaxed.

You have to discover yourself. But in order to discover yourself you have to find the path that leads you to relaxation. When you find it, the soul takes over automatically, completely transforming you. Soul is bliss, soul is ecstasy, and it is not limited to one thing. Soul can flow through everything. It can flow through compassion, through love, through mind, through everything and anything, but with one condition: you must be fully relaxed. If you are not relaxed, or if you are not aware, you will keep on missing the point.

Don't be calculating and don't have any ulterior motives, because if you do, relaxation will never happen. Be spontaneous in your actions and your soul will flow very easily. Then, when your soul is activated, love and compassion will have a totally different feeling. Trust yourself. Be spontaneous and be aware. Don't be calculating in your actions. When actions spontaneously flow from your heart, their healing power is directly generated from the soul. In such instances, merely observing a situation of pain can draw you into your soul, and compassion towards an individual or living being is transmitted, and their pain will be relieved. When compassion is true compassion, it creates an unbearable feeling in you, making you go to any extent to rid yourself of what you feel. Your actions will then not be generated by any recognition, but simply by your intensity to rid yourself of the pain you feel towards the situation without caring whether or not you get something in return.

In a deep state of relaxation, you will know where you stand and you will know that true love – true compassion – can only come from the heart, and not from your head. Love and compassion cannot be premeditated or they will lose all value. Love, for instance, is energy, and energy flows everywhere. How can you premeditate love? If you do, it will eventually crumble. If love is mind-oriented, it carries hate with it and will partake in duality. This kind of love can never be pure. But love which emanates from the heart has a spontaneous and clear nature. In fact, the more heart-oriented you are, the more pure and filled with love energy you will be. And when you are filled with love, your whole being will take on the appearance of emptiness. Have you ever observed a clear glass of water which is filled up to the rim? If you are aware, you will notice the glass will simultaneously take on both the qualities of fullness and of emptiness.

So don't do things for recognition, because if that is your goal, you will miss the real point altogether. If you try to get recognition, you will get it, but you will miss yourself. Your goal is to know yourself because only then will you know everything.

Seek right guidance. In the beginning, we all need right guidance. Be aware and make sure your guide appears like a clear glass of water with both the qualities of fullness and emptiness. If not, then search again until you find a guide with such qualities. Be relaxed, and all you ever wanted in life will come to you. Relaxation is the secret key to open the door of your being and to the whole.

SVARTHI

What is most important in this world? This question has been asked for centuries. Humans think that only human life is very important, but animals are not unhappy. Even a small bug crawling in the dirt is not unhappy. With his big body, an elephant is happy too. A little turtle lying in the mud is happy. The butterflies, the mosquitoes and the bees, all seem to be happy. So if all of nature is happy, why do I emphasize human life as being so important?

Human life is so important because humans have the ability to understand. To be born as human beings, we have already crossed a big ocean. But to discover yourself and to know who you *really* are, you have to go further. Now, you don't have to cross another ocean – just a little creek. You can cross it easily if you have the courage to take the leap. On the other side, everything will be crystal clear, all the curtains of illusion will fall automatically, all ignorance will vanish, and as a result, you will meet yourself for the first time. That's why we have the saying, "Human life is very important."

Human life is not important only by virtue of the fact that you are human. It is important in the sense that you have the ability to understand reality

55

and that you have to take advantage of this ability. In my opinion, humans don't seem to be using it. They're too content just staying where they are and they think that happiness is the most important thing to achieve. If this is what humans think, remember one thing: happiness is always followed by unhappiness. All of your virtues are followed by all of the sins, bad things follow all of your good things, and all good karma is followed by bad karma.

Duality is everywhere, and that's why it is so hard to cross this small creek. To cross it you have to go beyond duality. Even if you are not clinging to dualities such as happiness and unhappiness, virtue and sin, or good and bad, you are still clinging to something. Maybe you are clinging to God! You cannot get rid of clinging. You think it is wonderful to love God, but even loving God is duality. You have to go beyond duality to be able to explore your real Self. If you don't go beyond duality, real love will never flourish either.

You think that you are very loving because you love your family, you love your husband, you love your children, or even that you love your pets. But this love is not the kind of love I am talking about. The kind of love I am talking about is beyond duality, and for that you have to have courage to take the leap and cross this small creek.

Human beings in society are great experts in showing love. But because their love belongs to duality, they are missing the possibility to explore real love. Their love is self-motivated and it is used to convince themselves and others of their goodness. Have you ever heard an animal convincing his babies that they are loved? Or have you ever come across any animals constantly saying to their mates "I love you" as humans do?

In that realm, love is felt and that's why convincing is not needed. We as humans have lost these instinctive feelings. That's why we have to convince each other of our love.

I tell you that in our so-called "advanced society" we have to convince even little babies they are loved, otherwise the babies will not stop crying. The mother has to convince her child again and again of her love. In a way, you think that you love your family, but unless you know this kind of love, it means love is not inside of you. And if love is not inside of you, how can you love anybody? Forget about loving God: you don't even love yourself yet. God's love is a totally different phenomenon.

Fortunately, nature was very smart to create us in opposite sexes. In doing so, nature gave us a great opportunity. Our energies can attract each other as a way to learn love. The most important lesson in this universe is to learn the essence of what real love truly means. When opposite sexes attract each other, this attraction becomes the tool to learn the basic steps of love. It is from this first step that the journey to realize universal love starts. But most of our lives are lived in vain; we haven't really learned anything. We jump from here to there like monkeys jumping from one branch to another branch, from this tree to another tree, and from one relationship to another. But if instead of jumping from relationship to relationship we stay together and embrace each other fully, the chance to understand love's depth is increased a thousand-fold. When subtleties come to the surface, allow them, for they will take you deeper and deeper, all the way to the depth of your being. Flow with the river of love! Eventually you will reach the ocean, where you will silently dissolve and become one with universal love. But if you keep on jumping you will never have the chance to experience either silence or real love. You must come to a halt, and together look into your own selves and be each other's mirror. Then the possibility for real love can surface.

When love begins to grow inside of you, it shows that you have found the right way and you no longer have to convince anyone; even a child can feel loved now. When love is not inside of you, no one will feel it. But once love begins to really flow, whoever comes close to you will feel it. To have love inside oneself is the most important thing. When it happens, others will naturally sense it and will gravitate towards you.

Love has a beautiful aura, and once a person comes in its range it will be easily felt. God is attracted only by the aura of true love. Even if an artist, like Van Gogh, came back it would be to see what was once precious to them. Yes, he would come to see his beloved paintings, his creations, which is what he loved most in life. God too, loves to see his creations. So increase your aura of love and you will automatically attract God to you. God loves to come and see his creations and be part of your aura. Where there is real love, God has to come. But our way of love is not really love. Real love needs to be improved step by step.

Maybe in the beginning you might have to start with your own child or with your husband or your wife. But if you get stuck there your whole life, love will never have the chance to be explored. You will get fed up eventually. It is like eating the same bread, the same vegetable, or the same food every day. You will not like it and you will get bored unless your connection with your beloved can take you to your ultimate goal, which is to know your soul. If such a connection is not present, love will have no possibility to reach its depth and expand.

So in order for your love to shine, you have to expand your aura. Make it bigger and make it better. Even if you are staying with the same person, you will feel different. We need to expand the aura of love all the time. Love is basically the same, but once it is purified, it becomes divine, and when it becomes divine, it becomes Godly love. Godly love is totally different. A mother, if she is really a mother, will not only feel love for her own child, but for every child on Earth. If she only has love for her child, she really has not yet experienced motherhood. Even a guru has to experience true motherhood. This is how love expands slowly.

In a way, everybody is ours and in a way nobody is ours – even our own children are not ours. We expect that they are ours, but they are not. Once they have grown, they move away. They will have their own lives and you will have your own life. Maybe a friend is better to you than your children. Maybe your friend is willing to help you all the time, but your children are not. If love is really present in you, what you feel for your own child – or brother and sister – you will feel it in the same way for everybody. When love is explored to its fullest it becomes universal love, meaning you will be able to love not only your closest relations, but also every living being. You will feel love for trees, for mountains and for rivers. We need this kind of love. We need to love everything. This is the way to explore your Self. And if through your beloved you come close to this kind of love, you have reached the ultimate goal of life.

Look at a little seed. You put it in the ground and one day it will sprout and will become a tree. From that tiny seed you will get fruits. It is the same with humans. A little egg and a sperm meet, and soon they multiply from one cell to millions of cells. How does it happen? It is a mystery, and this mystery remains unsolved because we are satisfied to be where we are. We have no curiosity to go any further. Basically, there is no difference between you and animals. They are happy where they are. A little turtle is happy where he is, and you are happy where you are. You might say to me, "But I am a happy, successful doctor." Yes, you are happy because you love to live in such a small well. Actually, you are extremely content. But just to be content is not enough. If you are content to stay where you are you will never be able to realize the mystery of how life sprouts. Just imagine that out of a little sperm and a little egg life is born. You don't thirst to search the truth; you don't thirst to solve this mystery. You are basically content with happiness.

If you have no thirst, it means that you and a little bug are basically the same. A little bug enjoys his life and is even freer than you, maybe even more democratic than you. Maybe he has no king, no president, to rule over him. He does not have any government to pay taxes to. It seems that he is even better off than you. Maybe you are much lower than a bug! Think about it: at least a bug does not have a developed mind like you have.

Don't be content to remain where you are. You have to search further. This is what is so wonderful about human life. With human life you can search for the truth, and this is the reason why human life is so precious. Those people who begin to search are very fortunate and blessed people.

There is an Indian saying *"Chal manae chaliye,"* which means, "In taking a step, you are there." A similar saying in English is, "The journey of a thousand miles starts with a single step." But there is one condition: the step has to be taken in the right direction, on the right track. In practical life we also use the same words, but we don't pay any attention. If your husband has just left the house to go to New York and his friend calls for him, your reply will be, "He has gone to New York." Your husband just left the house and he is not even at the airport, but you still say he went to New York. So even in our practical life we say the same thing. But you don't pay attention to what you are saying. This is reality: if you take one step you have reached the destination already. But let me repeat it again: the step has to be in the right direction.

The importance of this life is to take the right step, to walk on the *right* track. Walking on the track is not what is important. Walking on the *right* track is important. When you are walking on the right track, you will feel as if there is a nice aura around you. When you do take the right step, you will be able to feel the aura of your being. It will shine and it will be very bright. It will be strong and it will increase your understanding. You will see yourself clearly as if you were a crystal ball. But first you have to take the right step and then you will know yourself.

But your fear stops you from taking the right step. You do not want to appear selfish in the eyes of others. People will think you are selfish if you devote your time searching your real Self. They will not like it, and will condemn you for your choice. All monks and all spiritual practitioners appear to be very selfish to others. Sometimes people say, "The only thing they do is sit and meditate; they don't do anything else."

In Japan, all that Zen monks do is to sit in meditation. In meditation, what do you do? Do you care about others? No. You are simply enjoying your consciousness. That seems selfish, and if you are selfish, how can you love others? How can you care about others? You can't because you are selfish. This is what you might think, but remember, this is not really selfishness. This is the only thing that can lead you somewhere. This selfishness one day will reveal your *being* fully. Unless this selfishness comes to you, you won't be able to reveal your Self – you won't be able to see yourself. Your being will remain covered by a thick curtain of ignorance. It is ignorance which prevents you from seeing, and which keeps you roaming in the dark all of the time. You have to be selfish in order to really love or to really care for the whole universe.

One day a scientist was walking and observing other planets with a big telescope. It was a perfect day to search and he did not want to miss this opportunity. All the planets were in the right alignment. He totally forgot everything around him and was just focused on his task. He was walking here and there when accidentally he bumped into an old lady. The poor woman fell down, but luckily she wasn't hurt. She asked the scientist, "Who are you?" He replied, "Stay out of my way. Can't you see I am searching for something? Today the sky is visible and I don't want to miss this opportunity. So don't block my way." The old lady replied, "My son, allow me to give you a suggestion. First, learn how to walk on Earth."

So in order to love others you have to be selfish. You have to first know how to walk on Earth. Unless you know yourself, you cannot know other people. In order to love other people, you must be selfish first. That's why all spiritual people seem to be very selfish. When I say selfish I mean you have to love yourself. In meditation – in *samadhi* – you have to go deeper and deeper into your being. Only if you can touch the bottom of your being will love for another then be possible.

Maybe you think you love because you have heard about it from your mother, from your sister, from your brother, or from your friends. Do you know that when two people fall in love for the first time they don't really know what to say to one another? Nowadays there are even schools where psychologists teach about love and how to deal with love. But if you cannot afford a psychologist, you ask your friend to help you because you don't know how to relate with your beloved. It means that your love doesn't come from the bottom of your being. You haven't revealed it to yourself yet – it is still hidden. You haven't touched your depths, and that's why you don't yet know how to be.

When love is fully open, it doesn't need words. Flowers do not force their perfume on anybody; they naturally give it away. But if your love needs to be proclaimed, it is merely ignorance. That's why it is so important that we awaken the love in our being. Once we know it, our job is done. It means that the step has been taken and your goal has been reached.

Remember, you have already come very far. Just by getting this human life you have crossed a big ocean, but the problem now is that you are stuck at the edge of the little creek refusing to jump over it for the fear of falling into it. To you it is like being in the Grand Canyon and the Colorado River running at the bottom. Even though the creek is not wide and you could jump it easily, your lack of courage prevents you from jumping.

Take the leap and you will reach the destination where you understand yourself. No matter what people think of you, don't worry about them. Don't search outside of yourself to find love; search inside of yourself first. Your thirst will lead you in the right direction. This is the selfishness I am talking about. Once you have found love inside of you, others will automatically feel it. It is just natural. If you don't know yourself, you cannot help anyone else. Our life is short. It may be seventy, eighty, even one hundred years, but one day it will be over. Even if you fix a date in the future, the end will come rapidly. The years will pass. One hundred years will seem like one moment at the end of your journey. So before you lose it, you better do something about it. Knowing yourself is the greatest goal of all. Take advantage now and do what it takes to reveal the hidden mystery inside of your being.

Be selfish and you will be able to love, to care, and to be a real help to everyone. If you try to help others before knowing yourself, your help will never be real help. Know pure love and you will know God and the mystery of life will be revealed to you. When you know yourself, you know everything. You will know your soul. This selfishness is something you really need to experience in order to love everything in the Universe. You have to be *svarthi*. "Sva" means "self," and "arthi" means "for it." Svarthi means "for the self." To know the self is the ultimate goal.

WHO AM I?

Everybody wants to know the answer to the question "Who am I?" But we focus only on our outer self, our body structures and our names. But if you want to introduce your mind and brain, is it possible? If I ask you who you really are, is it possible to answer truly? It would be very hard. The only thing you can tell about you is your name, your profession, your nationality and your family status. You can only convey your external self, and this too would be projection of mind. Beyond this, everything else is much too subtle to put into words. Can you imagine how much more difficult it would be to talk about the soul or your permanent and eternal Self? It is impossible to pass on to another person; it can only be realized.

Everything external is nothing more than borrowed knowledge, and no borrowed knowledge can help you to understand truth. No borrowed knowledge can help you to really find your Self. Your true Self goes beyond all borrowed knowledge. Any borrowed knowledge, like borrowed money, creates tension and worry over how to pay it back, and it will greatly disturb you mentally.

Just like money, your name, your body, and every external thing is borrowed, like your body has been borrowed from your parents. That's why sometimes we are very thankful to them. In fact, we should feel fortunate to have this body, because with this body we can experience reality. Even if this body is just borrowed, we should still be thankful for it.

So all borrowed things create problems, and the body is the first thing we encounter in the world which creates problems. It does not matter if it is the body, the mind or money. It does not matter what it is; we have borrowed it, and all borrowing in itself creates problems. Even your mere existence can hurt others, and your body is the first visible thing which can hurt another. You are not really *doing* anything to hurt people; you are not killing anyone, you are not purposefully hurting anyone's feelings or emotions, but your existence is hurting their feelings and their emotions. Let me give an example: I am walking on the beach, and by my nature I am very lovable and very compassionate to everybody, but people here do not like my white robes. In one way I am hurting them because they do not like my kind of clothing. I remember once I was walking in a city and four or five boys and girls were passing by. Seeing me, they started screaming, "Get the sheets off, get the sheets off!" I started laughing. I did not know them, but in a way I was hurting them; by merely existing I was hurting them.

So the body, because it is visible, becomes your first problem. Have you ever heard of angels hurting others? Why not? What is their secret or mystery? There is no secret or mystery. You simply haven't heard anything because an angel's body is invisible, not visible like yours. They have astral bodies, and astral bodies are like air. You can feel them but cannot see them. So merely by having a body, we involuntarily hurt others. I suggest you never hurt anyone deliberately. But if you learn to be silent and compassionate, your existence might hurt much less. Remember that if anyone feels you have hurt them, it is only because of ignorance.

If one thinks, "I don't like that person," know that it is merely ignorance talking. But if he or she realizes how compassionate and how full of love that person is, he or she might change their mind and realize it is not nice to think certain thoughts about another person. Also, if at the other end you get hurt, this too is because of ignorance. If you want to experience reality, you have to remove your ignorance. Ignorance is like a cloud that hides the sun. The sun is still shining, but the cloud is too thick to allow any sun-rays to shine through. When the cloud is too thick, not a single ray can reach the Earth. Ignorance is like a cloud. It is like pollution and like snow and you cannot see anything when surrounded by it. You are in complete darkness. This is the reason why I tell you to remove this type of cloud. The sun is always shining; you only need to remove the cloud of ignorance, which in Sanskrit is referred to as *maya*. Maya is like darkness and it means "illusion." My suggestion is not to "get the sheets off," but to get rid of darkness. If you really get rid of darkness, you will be able to see your sun: you will see your soul.

Your soul is like the sun – it is always shining – but because clouds, darkness, ignorance and lower qualities cover it, you are not able to see it. So remove your lower qualities. But you ask me, "How can I remove this darkness?" Let me tell you, this is the most wonderful question you could have asked. There are many paths. If there are many clouds in the sky, there are also many ways to get rid of them. For example, if there is a strong wind, clouds cannot stay. So you must create some wind. But what kind of wind do I need to create? The wind of compassion, of truth, of non-violence. If you truly ask me, I say the wind of "love." Love comes from inside, and with real love, even when a person says to you, "I hate you," your love can still flow towards that person. This is the kind of love I am talking about. So you need this type of love, very strong love. And love in my opinion is always strong.

In Hindi there is a wonderful verse: "Oh my friend, if you really want to understand and want to learn what love is, you need to understand the sugar cane, then you can know what real love is." Chew a piece of sugar cane and you will find that where there is hardness, there is no juice. The juice is only on the soft part of the cane. So our great saints taught us that if you really want to learn love, you learn from the sugar plant. Where there is softness there is love, but where there is hardness you find no love there.

So where there is hardness, where there is violence, where someone is telling lies or someone wants to hurt someone, love is no longer there. So when the wind of love blows, all clouds of ignorance will be removed too. Illusion does not have any other alternative; it cannot stand such strong wind.

But you need real love, natural love, not artificial love. You can make love artificial by polishing it, but this love will only work for a while. It will not last forever. You have to find the way to develop real love. When a boy or girl feels love, they will try to seduce each other. Maybe they are not feeling love yet, but they still say how much they love: "I really love you, I love you so much." He or she praises the other a lot, but it means that they are polishing love. This type of love will not last forever; it will only last for a short time. But if you have real love, you don't need to say anything. You get together, sit together, maybe you are even silent, but you feel so much for each other. Sometimes if you have real love you can suddenly enter into meditation. There are so many stories about this kind of love, like Romeo and Juliet. In India there are also many stories like this. The two lovers die but people still worship them. Sometimes they have never even gotten together, but still they had real love.

Love, which is eternal and natural and which exists forever, is considered to be the real food for the soul. Increase all the things which can feed the soul. Once your soul becomes stronger and heavy on your mind, your energy will no longer be scattered here and there. The energy which is right now scattered in desires, in deceiving others, in criticizing others, or pulling down others, in killing others, or simply scattered everywhere will no longer be scattered because the soul is now heavy on the mind. When the soul is heavy on the mind you will feel something unique inside of you as if you have suddenly been transformed. Then your curiosity, which was alive in your childhood, will start again. By the way, if you ask yourself the question "Who am I?" this is not considered to be curiosity. It is the real way to get to know your soul.

Increase these types of qualities. Feed your soul with compassion, sympathy, and truth. Don't be egoistic or proud and you will be able to see your energy, which was before scattered here and there, becoming concentrated. Once your energy is concentrated, your power will increase. The sun has much power too, but if the rays are not concentrated they will have limited power. Concentrate them and their power can burn anything.

You have as much power, and this is why I tell you that you have infinite power, but you are not familiar with who you really are. You have to consider yourself from the very beginning, from even before you entered your mother's womb. Before that you were traveling. If you were not traveling, you could not enter your mother's womb. So don't think this is your first life. Right now, you are still traveling, but in another way you are trying to realize yourself. This time, make sure you travel with good people, with nice people, and maybe you will not get tired or bored.

Sometimes after coming back from your job, you feel so tired. Have you ever asked yourself why? Maybe you did not really like what you were doing, or maybe you were not around people who are positive thinkers. If this is the case, it means you were not traveling with the right people. But if you are around your favorite friends, maybe you spend all night in their presence, talking and laughing, and after many hours you still feel fresh. Why were you not tired then? It means you were traveling with friendly people, with positive thinkers. So if you will travel with positive thinkers, good people, nice people, great men, then you will enjoy your travels. So make good friends, make connections with great people. People are always searching for good people.

In India many people seek the company of monks because they know that monks are good, unselfish and compassionate. For this reason people sometimes travel with them. In fact, there is a special Jain sect where the monks travel barefoot from village to village, and people enjoy walking with them. If they walk with the monks, people feel they have much opportunity to learn many things. At times, even one sentence can make a big difference to the person walking in the company of a monk. What you are learning in walking, especially in the company of a self-realized person, might not have the same effect if you are merely reading the same thing in a book. Besides, walking is good exercise. So when you are physically fresh, you are also mentally fresh. My suggestion to you is to travel with good people, positive people, and maybe then you will enjoy your journey. This life is a journey and if you really want to enjoy this journey, make sure you have good connections. Otherwise you will be very bored.

Have you ever seen a dying person? They suffer a lot because they are not ready to leave this body. They want to live longer and they are not ready to leave because their journey has not really been fulfilling. They insist on being saved so they can have another chance to at least try to enjoy their journey. But if you really had enjoyed your journey you would probably celebrate the fact that you are leaving this body. And if your journey was completely fulfilled, you would leave with no regrets at all. If you surround yourself with positive thinkers, when the end comes you will not ask to be saved.

I just remembered a story: a person was walking by the bank of the river when accidentally he fell into the river. He did not know how to swim and he was drowning. One person walking by heard him say, "I am drowning, I am drowning, please help me." The man walking by replied, "If you are drowning, just drown – drowning does not need help."

You still have time, so start your journey now and surround yourself with positive thinking people. If you do so, when the end of your journey comes you will have no regrets. Once natural death occurs it will be a real celebration for you. When you can really celebrate, then you cannot forget this life. And whenever you will travel, whenever you will find vacancy and enter another womb, you will remember your previous life; you will be able to remember everything. This is very important, because if we can remember a previous life we can avoid repeating the same mistakes. So live simply but practice elevated thinking, and one day you can achieve high consciousness. Then, and only then, you will come to know who you really are.

MEDITATION

Meditation is a very simple phenomenon, but very difficult to achieve. Meditation is not something you do. Meditation is something you get. Whenever you try to meditate, meditation never happens. Meditation means effortlessness state of consciousness.

When everything is loosened, relaxed and forgotten, meditation happens. Meditation is the highest peak of consciousness and if you can achieve the highest peak of consciousness, you have achieved enlightenment. Enlightenment means no worries, no disturbances, no pain, no misery, no suffering, pure joy, ecstasy, and bliss.

Remember these important statements:

Tamaso Ma Jyotir Gamaye.
Mrityor Ma Amritam Gamaye.
Asato Ma Sad Gamaye.

Meditation will always bring you from darkness to light.
Meditation will always bring you from death to bliss and ecstasy.
Meditation will always bring you from mortality to immortality.

73

Man is mortal because his body is mortal. The body does not stay forever. Everybody knows it deep down, but nobody is really accepting this truth. You don't know how fortunate you are to have this human life. Human life gives you the possibility to open your consciousness. But remember, it is only a possibility.

Jesus said, "I am the door, pass through me." Actually, this is the most wonderful statement made on Earth. "I am the door, pass through me." But people have misunderstood this wonderful statement. They understood Jesus to be the door through which you had to pass. This is not what Jesus meant. Jesus meant human life is the door. Human life is the door to the eternal. Your body is the door to enter into the kingdom of God. No wonder we are in trouble. We have completely missed the real meaning of human life.

You think that this body is just the combination of five elements: air, space, fire, earth and water. It is not so. This body is much more than that. The body is a great instrument. If you know the science of the body, you will come to understand its language also. To understand your body is to make it pure, and only in a pure body can God dwell and sing its tune.

Human life is so important and so precious because only with human life can mind be really developed. A well-developed and sharp mind is essential for self-exploration. It can explore itself in different directions in order to realize truth. Mind can realize that this is not right for me. This is not for me, and that this is not who I am. No matter if I earn millions of dollars, money is not who I am. No matter how big of a house or palace I have, a house or a palace is not who I am. No matter how beautiful, big or fast my car is, a car is not who I am. No matter if I can create thousands of paintings, paintings are not who I am. Actually, a developed mind can go even a step further. It can question itself by asking: "Who am I?" It is a very simple question, but powerful. Such a question, when asked, can instigate the mind to realize the truth. Let me tell you, such a simple question can really awaken you to truly know who you really are. Pass through your body and you will find the answer.

You are not separate from this truth. This truth is *you*. It just needs to be realized. The truth of the "real you" is hidden in your body like butter is hidden in the milk and it cannot be revealed by merely thinking or praying on it. By just praying, can you get the butter out of the milk? No you can't, and you know it. You have to know the process of how to get it. You cannot see the butter because it is not visible, but if you know the process you will have butter too. Prayer alone will not help you to get the butter. Sit in front of the milk and pray to God to turn milk into butter and you might be really disappointed.

God only helps those who help themselves. You have been praying for centuries, maybe even for hundreds of lives. You have already wasted hundreds of lives with your prayers. Has God ever turned the milk into butter for you? No, you are still waiting. God helps only those who help themselves. Learn the process and God will turn the milk into butter. Find your Self, and then prayer will be helpful. Remember, you are more important than prayers. If you know your Self, you know the process, and if you know the process, you can get whatever you want.

You are important: always remember this. Even Jesus pointed out that you are very important. Jesus told you, "You are the door, pass through it." Only when you understand the process can meditation, the highest state of consciousness, be realized.

Don't waste this life. Get started and go deep, find the process. Don't waste any more time. Maybe if you pass through your body, to work on yourself, maybe meditation could happen. It could happen tomorrow, it could happen today, or even right now as I speak. Glimpses of truth can descend suddenly. They are all around you. They surround you all the time, but something is blocking them from reaching you.

A few days ago I was telling a very enlightening story. Twenty-six hundred years ago, Mahavira, one of India's well-known prophets, had a chief disciple named Gautama. Gautama was like his shadow. Gautama was always following him. No matter where he was going, Gautama was following him. Wherever Mahavira sat, Gautama sat close to him. Gautama listened to every lecture he gave. For twenty-eight years, Gautama followed Mahavira constantly. Gautama was a scholar and he knew all the scriptures and every holy book. Gautama had surrendered himself fully to his teacher. No matter where Mahavira sent him, Gautama would go. Gautama helped many of Mahavira's disciples to achieve enlightenment while he himself still couldn't achieve it. Mahavira would send him places and people would be awakened by simply hearing him. Just by talking to them and just by touching them they will get enlightened.

One day, Mahavira and Gautama were walking together. Mahavira suggested to Gautama that just ten miles away, in a nearby village, there were five hundred monks who really wanted to know the truth. Somehow

76

they were partially enlightened but not fully. Their consciousness was open enough to clearly see seven oceans and seven galaxies. For years they had been preaching that these seven oceans and seven galaxies were the whole universe. Mahavira instructed Gautama to go there and introduce himself to them and ask them the question: how big is this universe? Mahavira knew that by this question all of them would be confused, and that in their confusion they would enquire even more. Gautama didn't want to leave his master, but he knew he had to go, so he left. The five hundred monks were all involved in their spiritual practices. As soon as they noticed Gautama, they greeted him with respect. They asked him where he was coming from, and whom was he following. Gautama replied, "I don't know, but my Lord is always with me."

After a short dialog, Gautama enquired a little more and asked the question – "How big is this universe?"   All together they answered: "Seven oceans, seven galaxies, and nothing else." Gautama told them, "But my Lord always says that there are millions of galaxies." "Did he say millions of galaxies? Amazing!" they said. From his question, all the five hundred monks started wondering, and as soon as they started wondering, all of their knowledge disappeared too. Their light was gone.

Whenever there is wonder, light leaves and confusion enters. All of a sudden they were in complete darkness. "What are we going to do now?" they asked each other. "Oh! Don't worry," answered Gautama, "I will make you my disciples and you will achieve enlightenment."

They all thought Gautama was incredible. "He confused us…we were in the light, and now we are all in darkness again." They accepted his idea and followed him like sheep and walked with him to meet his master.

After walking barely one mile, Gautama began to instruct them and told them what they had to do once they reached his master. "Once we are there, you will go directly to my Lord and you will bow to him. He will be easily recognized because he shines so much. On his right side there are hundreds of enlightened monks. Bow to them too. In the third row, behind them, there are more monks, and you will sit there with them."

They all agreed to do as they were instructed. In the meantime, along the way, something happened to all of the five hundred monks. All together they started thinking the same old thoughts and began to repeat: "For many years we were preaching and instructing people about the seven oceans, seven galaxies and nothing else. We have been lying to people all of our lives, when we ourselves couldn't see the whole truth clearly." Collectively, they started thinking how wrong they had been and they began to realize that the whole truth was something else. They thought over and over it even more deeply and they came to know that they were absolutely wrong. They thought, "Light would not have disappeared if we knew the truth. It means we didn't know ourselves yet."

On the way they were very deeply focused on themselves. After walking one more mile, Gautama again reminded them that they had to bow to the Lord, to bow to the enlightened monks sitting to the right side of the Lord, and to sit in the third row by the other monks. They all replied, "Yes, we will remember it." In the meantime, as they were walking, deep in their hearts they were really repenting and focusing on themselves, and all of a sudden they were thrown into their original center and became totally balanced, and after few more minutes they achieved enlightenment.

Now they could see everything clearly, and the full universe became very apparent. As they began to approach the master, Gautama reminded them once again of their duties. When they finally arrived, the moment was incredible. They immediately recognized the Lord. He was shining. At once they bowed down to him. But when they got to the enlightened monks, instead of bowing down to them, they sat with them. Gautama, the chief disciple, became very confused by their behavior, and began to doubt even his own master. His master had told him that he would be the one to bring them to enlightenment. Instead, they couldn't even understand and follow a little discipline and refused to follow his instructions completely. He started thinking, "Look at them, all the way from that village to here I kept telling them not to sit by the enlightened monks. But they are so ignorant, they couldn't even follow this much instruction."

As he was thinking this way, Mahavira, his master, pointed out to him his own thoughts and said, "Gautama! What is going on in your mind? You think that they are ignorant and they don't understand your instructions. Gautama, you are not aware that they too have become enlightened. Right now they know everything. It is you who still doesn't know." Gautama started crying like a baby and said to Mahavira: "I have been with you for twenty-eight years. You have sent me everywhere and I have awakened many people. Why am I not attaining enlightenment? Why?" Mahavira pointed out to Gautama that his attachment to his Lord was preventing him from being enlightened.

Now think about it...if Gautama's attachment to his enlightened master blocked him from reaching enlightenment, what will happen to you when you are still filled with so many more attachments? You are attached to things. If you are attached to your property, to your money, to your jewelry, to your clothes, to people, and to all of the worldly things, how can you achieve enlightenment?

Mahavira then pointed out to Gautama: "As long as you are attached to me, you never will achieve enlightenment." You are always saying, 'My Lord says this, my Lord says that.' In your mind there is always 'my' and you are so attached to me as if I am your possession. You have to understand that until you are totally free from attachment, you cannot achieve enlightenment." Mahavira continued, "I also know that as long as I'm still alive you cannot achieve enlightenment. You cannot keep yourself away from me." And it is true that Gautama never became enlightened until his master left his last body.

Many things block your consciousness, but your biggest enemy is your attachment to worldly things – to people and to God. You know it already; it is just a matter of time. If you are attached to someone, one day he or she might leave you or you might leave him or her. We are all standing in a big line waiting for our turn. You might go first or I might go first, but one thing is sure…our turn will come sooner or later. We will all have to go. Maybe it will take fifty years or sixty years or even one hundred years, but your turn will come for sure.

I read in a book about an incredible thing. A *chakravarti*, a person who ruled all over the world, was already ruling half of the world. He wanted to conquer the other half so he could be the ruler of the whole world. In between the side he ruled over and the other side there was a big cave. In front of the cave there was a big rock, which was very difficult to remove. The chakravarti put forth his whole effort by engaging the help of all of his elephants, all of his horses, and even all of his army. But any attempt was in vain. Not only could it not be removed, it couldn't even be moved a little. Suddenly, the chakravarti came up with another idea, which successfully removed the rock. He became very happy and he started jumping up and down with joy saying: "I am the only one to rule over the whole world."

But before crossing the cave he thought it would be a great idea to sign his name all over the cave to make everyone aware that he was the only one ruling over the whole world. He was bubbling with happiness, but his happiness was short-lived. To his surprise, as he lit the cave, he could not find even a single space available for his signature. The whole cave was already filled with names. He had wanted to be the only one. Instead, he found that he had many predecessors already. Many had passed through the cave long before he did.

Think about it: even your name does not belong to you. Your parents have given it to you. Once a person leaves the body, the name will be gone too. In history there are only two kinds of people, either good people or evil people, and both kinds of people are equally remembered. In the case of evil people, no one ever thinks of naming their children after them. Their names are merely remembered so as not to repeat the same mistake again. But the names of good people are often passed on. If you want to be remembered, collect lots of good energy right now so that your name too can be remembered in history, otherwise once your life ends nothing will be left of you.

You have been fortunate to have this body, but if you don't utilize this instrument or this door, you will have wasted the most precious opportunity. You don't know how soon you can get this instrument back again. That's why this instrument is very, very important. Utilize it and use it correctly. Collect good energy and open your consciousness. Start today to realize your Self. Soon you will understand the whole truth. In achieving the highest peak of consciousness, meditation is achieved.

SUBTLE BODY

Yes, this body can age, but this is not really aging. Aging is a totally different phenomenon. In Indian mythology there is a saying: "The being - the soul - never dies." It is the container which houses the soul that changes. It is like changing clothes. It is used for a period of time just as we do with our clothes. Here, however, I am talking about something else... I am referring to the subtle body.

The subtle body is the bridge between the soul and the gross body. When I say gross body, I mean the physical body - with bones, muscle, marrow, tendons, veins, etc. It is inside this gross body that we can find the subtle body. It is not visible but you can feel it. It is like an angel's body. Many people say that angels appear. They are not visible but you can feel them. Angels have a light body, like air. You can feel their presence but you cannot catch them because they are not touchable. Even light is not visible; light enables us to see things, but light itself is not visible. Angels' bodies are like that, and subtle bodies are even subtler than light bodies.

In the Jain religion, one of the oldest religions in India, the subtle body is called *Karman Sharir*. Karman is that mechanism which takes pictures and collects karma. Therefore, it is psychologically and scientifically true that whatever we sow we reap the results of accordingly. Take anger, for example. If we flow in anger, the emotion of anger creates and releases certain atoms which automatically attach themselves to the subtle body. But if we flow in compassion and love, other kinds of particles will be attracted and attached to our subtle body.

The subtle body works like a camera. When you use the camera to take a picture, you cannot see the picture being taken. You can see the negative and after the film had been developed you see the picture. Even though you never saw the picture coming into the camera, the camera still recorded the picture. Nothing is visible, at least until after the film has been processed. The same goes for Karman Sharir; you can only see the results. Karman is the camera that takes the pictures. It is like the silicon chip that stores all the information in a computer. Sharir means simply "body," while Karman Sharir is one kind of subtle body in which all karmas are stored. This specific subtle body works just like the analogy of the camera.

Sometimes the subtle body can also work through dreams. It is rare, yet it is possible, that a person can be awakened through dreams. It is a possibility because in dreams there are no restrictions. This is why many people do dream therapy. Freud seemed to think that seeing a fish in a dream represents your sexuality. Or maybe that you feel love for a person. But this is only Freud's interpretation. It does not mean this theory is correct. I will suggest to you that if you see a fish it means good luck. Good luck can come in different ways. It can flow in prosperity, money or towards a person you love. It can also be about your child. So you can be awakened in a dream, but it is a rare phenomenon.

During sleep, so many things can go on. Through certain instruments you can record the brainwave activity that goes on during sleep. This is why it is important to develop our awareness. Whether you are awake or asleep, your subtle body goes on taking pictures all the time. If you are dreaming of killing someone, don't think that you will be exonerated. You will still get bad results because Karman Sharir goes on taking pictures, even if it is only a dream. Can you be that aware? Sometimes people are aware even in their dreams. They start thinking about their actions and feel it is not good to kill anyone. If they start thinking through the dream it means there is some awareness. This is why awareness is very important.

Buddha, the Enlightened One, once was walking with his disciple when he felt that something was on his shoulder. Automatically, he moved his hand to the shoulder to push it away. It was a fly, and luckily the fly did not die, and it flew away. Soon after, Buddha repeated the same gesture. As Buddha was repeating the same gesture, his disciple asked, "The first time your hand moved because there was a fly, but why did you repeat the same action a second time?" Buddha responded, "For a moment I was not aware that I could have killed the fly. I was not aware the first time, which is why I am repeating the same action because this time I am doing it with awareness."

When there is awareness you will never collect karma. Your subtle body will not collect any atoms or particles. Karman Sharir will take no pictures. Anger is a bad particle; compassion is a good particle. Either way, it still keeps you connected to this gross body. You will die and be reborn over and over until your awareness develops and you no longer collect karma. As long as the subtle body keeps taking pictures because of a lack of awareness, you will continue to take birth after birth. The key is to witness your actions so you do not collect karma. Be a witness. Witness all of your actions and activities. How can you be angry if you are witnessing? You might be unaware momentarily, but as soon as you realize what you are doing, you begin to be a witness.

Being a witness is the key. Witnessing is like a strong sun which melts the ice. As soon as the sun rises, the ice melts. The same thing happens when you become a witness. Witnessing will melt the subtle body. In Hindi it is called *tapascharya* or *tapasya* ("austerity"), but this concept has been misunderstood. People would merely go out in the hot sun and start damaging their own bodies. Buddha did it, and Mahavira did it too, but when they did it they did it as an experiment which was done with awareness. If you go to India you see so many monks standing in the sun on one foot, torturing themselves. If this body is being tortured it automatically means there is no awareness. This body has nothing to do with *moksha* or liberation. It is the subtle body that needs to melt. Only when the sun rises high can ice be melted. So only when witnessing rises high can the subtle body be dissolved. When you become a witness, you will be aware of every little action. If you can witness every action, that witnessing will melt your subtle body. And when your subtle body has melted, then the soul can see the body.

In the Sankhya system there is a five thousand year-old technique. This system says that when the *purush*, which is the soul or the being, sees the *prakriti* (gross material, or gross body), it means that your subtle body has melted already. After Buddha was enlightened, someone asked, "What happens with enlightenment?" Buddha replied by saying, "My home melted, it is destroyed. It was with me for centuries and now it is fully, fully gone." He was referring to the subtle body, the bridge that connects the gross body to the soul. Once the subtle body is gone, it means you have achieved moksha, or liberation. You can be in moksha even though the physical body is still with you. This state of being is called *Jivan-Mukati*.

You will know when your subtle body is melting. I will give you a simple example. Think of those times when you are standing in a draft. The wind is cold, the sun is setting, and you are not protected with the proper attire. All of a sudden you feel the coldness penetrating you, going deep into your bones. You know then and there that a cold is imminent. You could not see it coming, but you know it has entered you. The same is true with the subtle body. When it melts, you know it is melting. You feel it going further and further down and once it is dissolved, moksha happens. Only at the time when a person feels that the subtle body is melting can he or she predict that this is their last journey or last body. If you are not having the experience it cannot be predicted whether this will be your last journey or your last body.

You need to work on your subtle body. But you need not to forget your gross body in the process. The physical body is also very important and you need to work on it because if this body is not healthy it will be impossible to then be sensitive to the subtle body. You need to take very good care of this body. Once this body becomes sensitive, you might be sensitive to your subtle body too. But don't forget which is the real body. Always remember that the gross body is not the real body; the subtle body is.

In Hindi, *Maha Mrityu* means moksha and it happens only once. We die only once. Really, Christianity is right to say there is no rebirth. What it doesn't specify is the fact that if we die without awareness we will be reborn. Dying without awareness keeps us from remembering our past life. When you die with awareness, all the memories are brought forth into the next life. Christianity, unknowingly, told the truth when it said "you die only once." Maybe Jesus, when he was in India for those eighteen years, learned these ideas and taught that in dying with awareness there is no more rebirth, only moksha. You can learn these ideas too. Try to work on your body to make it as sensitive as possible so that through developing sensitivity the subtle body can be dissolved. And you can achieve nirvana, the moksha.

MAHAVIR JAYANTI

This year marks the twenty-six hundredth birthday of Lord Mahavira.

Lord Mahavira was a blessing to humanity. Even before his birth his coming was considered to be a miracle. From his parents to the whole kingdom, everyone benefited from his coming and every person felt he was the reason behind all the sudden changes. Prosperity and riches rapidly propagated throughout the kingdom. This is why he was named *Vardhman*, as homage to him. Vardhman means "a person that is growing." The whole kingdom became very rich and gained more and more treasures. Diseases were disappearing rapidly. Everything flourished wildly and luck became a tangible experience to everyone.

As a child, Mahavira was extraordinary. He was a genius and knew so much. He used to pose such questions that not even his teacher knew the answers. He was so brilliant! The teacher would often compliment his father for having been blessed with such an extraordinary son. The teacher repeatedly told Mahavira's father that his son had to be born enlightened already. For this very reason the father renamed him *Sanmati*, meaning "genius one."

According to the Shwetambar sect of Jains, Mahavira married but soon after his marriage he decided to renounce the world and fully dedicated his life solely to spiritual practice. He wanted to show the light to everyone. It was after he left his kingdom that he became "Mahavira." Mahavira means "the very brave person, the bravest one." He was also known as Ati Veer, meaning "no comparison" - he was so brave. Eventually Mahavira attained *Keval Jnan*, full enlightenment, and soon after he began to spread his message to everyone all over the kingdom. Non-violence became his main principle, and to "be thankful to everyone" was his first lesson.

Merely not to kill any living being on its own is not what non-violence really means. I am stressing living beings including animals, vegetables, and anything that is alive - bacteria too. Can you imagine bacteria being a life form? Do you know that if you do not eat bacteria you will not survive? Those little bacteria are doing something for you. Actually, you are alive because of them, and you have never been thankful even once to them. So learn and be thankful to everyone.

Can you imagine if there were no oxygen? You wouldn't be alive without it. Oxygen carries lots of bacteria, and in just one breath you might swallow millions of bacteria. Have you ever stopped for a moment to be thankful to all those bacteria? Or have you ever stopped to think how many breaths you have taken in twenty-four hours? Do you know that in the period of twenty-four hours you take almost twenty-one thousand eight hundred and sixty breaths? So Mahavira's first teaching was: "Be thankful to every living being, because of them you survive." Maybe because of you they survive too: *Parasparopgraho jivanam* means coexistence. You live because of them, they live because of you.

I was in Chicago once and I visited a museum. I saw that on top of a glass container these words were written: "Surviving because of each other." Coexisting inside a hermetically sealed container there was a little snake and a little plant keeping each other alive. The little snake needed oxygen to survive, while the little plant needed carbon dioxide in order to survive. It reminded me of Mahavira's teaching and of his slogan: *Paras parop graho jivanam,* meaning live and let live, or coexistence.

So Mahavira's teaching of non-violence does not only mean not to kill, it also means to feel oneness with every living being. He asks, "If you feel oneness with your own child, why don't you feel the same oneness with other children too? Or if you feel oneness with your own pet, why don't you feel the same oneness with all the other pets?" Do you feel oneness with other living beings? If you don't, Mahavira says you are not doing the right thing. If you fully want to be non-violent you must feel oneness with every living being. Feel it with the trees, feel it with the rocks, feel it with the stars, and feel it with the whole universe. If you feel it with the whole universe, then the real non-violence starts.

Gandhi adopted this same principle and insisted never to compromise with violence, no matter what. Even if someone hits you, do not hit back. Non-violence is the most significant principle in Indian culture and their slogan is *Ahimsa Parmo Dharma*, meaning "non-violence is the best way of life." This is the first motto and it is written in every school and college. Wherever you go you will see it.

Actually, non-violence is the greatest principle on Earth. Without non-violence, you cannot survive. Can you imagine if all the trees and vegetation disappeared from this Earth? What would happen to you? I will tell you what would happen: you would disappear too. You never think this way, do you? Be thankful to all the vegetation and to the oxygen they provide you.

In Indian culture, it is thought to worship nature even before God. And in the Vedas, the very first books written in the whole world, it is written to worship the sun, the stars, the moon, and nature as a whole before anything else. I think if you could learn that you would be the best person on this planet.

You must first learn to love yourself, otherwise how can you love others? If you do not feel attuned with yourself, how can you be attuned with others? First, I suggest your charity begin at home. Everything starts from you. If you do not feel love, even for yourself, how can you feel love for other people? You have to feel love for your body, for your soul, for whatever is yours. You must consider your body to be the temple of the living God. You must keep your body healthy and your mind clean. If you want your prayer to be heard you must pray with a clean mind. If your mind is dirty, even if you pray for twenty-four hours, your prayer will never be heard. So even if you pray for two minutes, it is best that you pray with a clean and pure mind.

We need to keep in mind Mahavira's principles. His first principle is non-violence. The second principle, which I happen to really like, is *anekantvada*, meaning "multiplicity of truth." Truth cannot be told. Even if we try, it cannot be told. As soon as we speak, it becomes a lie. But Mahavira's seven steps at least teach us that truth can be analyzed. This principle is called *syadvada*, meaning "seven steps." From where I stand, my interpretation of truth might differ from yours. You are seeing it from a different angle. If from my side I see black, form your side you might see white. So should we fight over who is right? We are both right according to our perspectives, so there is no need to fight over it. At the same time we are also both wrong because one angle cannot encompass the whole truth.

Mahavira taught his first principle in his childhood. One day he was in his palace, standing on the third floor when his friend came to visit him. Mahavira heard his voice and said, "Come, I am up here on the third floor." His friend went up but instead of reaching the third floor he went to the fourth one. So now Mahavira was down below him instead of being up above him. His mother was confused and said, "Why did you say you were up when you are down below him?" Depending on where you stand in relation to another, your position might shift from upward to downward and vice versa. This is why Mahavira says that at the same time all the qualities are present in us. If goodness is present now, in the next moment badness can appear. If we are higher one moment, we can be low the next, and so on.

Anekantvada starts from here. Somehow, the smallest finger in my hand is not absolutely the smallest one even though it seems it is. Maybe in my hand it is the smallest, but if I compare it to someone else with a smaller hand than mine, his smaller fingers will be smaller than mine. Mine will no longer be the smallest. So my smallest finger has both qualities of being smaller and at the same time bigger.

But you see only one side, and truth is not one sided. Truth has many angles; however, we try to analyze truth from one angle and this is why we are wrong.

Lao-Tse said, "Truth cannot be told." But Mahavira said if you have these seven steps, *Sapt Bhangi, Sydvada*, you might be able to analyze it. Even one simple aspect of the truth ought to be analyzed by these seven steps. When you can do this there will be no reason to fight over anything any more. This tape recorder I am speaking into is black, but you cannot absolutely be sure it is black. Take it and put it in the sun, and after some time it will have faded, and it will no longer be quite as black. This means that your truth has become a lie already. It is best if you add, "At this time, this tape recorder seems black." This is the way to phrase your words, otherwise you are always wrong. How can you tell that something is white? Right now it seems white, but it can change. After a while it might get a yellow tinge or even a black tinge. So whatever is now is no longer the case some time from now. Everything changes very rapidly.

Somehow, everyone is right according to their angle, but if they learn the multiplicity of truth, people never will fight each other. The mother-in-law will never fight with her daughter-in-law. A daughter will not fight with her mother. A son will not fight with his father because they will have learned the multiplicity of truth. And by learning not to say "never" or "only," a lot of difficulties can be prevented.

Mahavira simply said that if you use the word *bhi*, meaning "too" or "also" instead of using *hi,* meaning "this is it," fighting can be prevented. Instead of saying, "That's the only way," say, "This can also be possible." If you speak as if this is the only way or the only thing available, know that you have already closed all possibilities for seeing the whole truth. You must be open to all available possibilities. So by using *too* or *also,* you have opened yourself to more options.

Truth has many different angles, all of which can be right. This can be a possibility, but at the same time something else can also be possible. Where something becomes an absolute truth and gives no chance to see the other side, inevitably, fights happen. You must be able to see all the different angles; maybe the other point of view contains its own truth also. Even five different points of view might all be telling the truth. None might be absolute, but can be partially related. Even in lying you can find a bit of truth. Similarly, in telling truth, you might find a bit of a lie.

Let me tell you a story. There was a person who lived in a small village and he used to tell lies all the time. Even though he was a perpetual liar, he still possessed popularity among the villagers. His lies seemed to be truths. One day a simple and innocent man considered becoming like the liar, and he thought to himself, "I am always telling the truth, but no one respects me as they respect him – why? Maybe I too will lie like he does." So one day when the people were gathered for a special occasion he announced that he heard dogs barking in the sky. He did not know what else to say, so he fabricated this lie. Everyone started laughing at him. "It is impossible, you are lying," everyone shouted. "We did not know you were such a liar, but now we know that you are." The poor fellow was heartbroken. Not only did he get no respect, but he was insulted too. He couldn't even go out of his house because he was so ashamed of himself.

In the meantime, the real liar who was gone out of town for a month came back to the town. He happened to see that poor fellow and saw that he was really weak looking, so he asked him why he was feeling so low. "I tried to imitate you, but look at me now. I cannot even show my face in the streets," said the man. "What happened?" asked the real liar. "I tried to be like you by declaring I heard dogs barking in the sky!" said the man. "Do not worry," the liar said, "I can prove you were right." "I would be very thankful to you if you could do this for me," said the man. "Please prove it." "I will," the real liar replied. As soon as the occasion presented itself, and once all the people were gathered, the liar announced, "Listen everyone, I heard dogs barking in the sky." "Oh! A second liar," the people replied. "No," he said, "Listen, I really heard it. It really happened." "How?" the villagers asked. "It happened this way," he uttered. "There was a female dog that just had puppies. Nearby a cow was also giving birth." "Alright, we understand. But how is it possible to hear dogs barking in the sky?" asked the crowd. The liar explained, "Well, after the cow delivered her little baby calf, the placenta was expelled from her stomach. The puppies were roaming around her, and when the placenta fell from the cow, two puppies got caught in it. Not only one puppy got trapped, but two puppies got caught in it!" The people were listening very attentively to what he was saying. "Yes, it is possible," they were murmuring. "Still, we do not understand how you could have heard puppies barking in the sky." The liar further explained, "What really happened after that? There was a big vulture flying overhead and you know vultures really love to eat anything. So the vulture came and picked up the placenta, including the puppies that were stuck under it, and flew away. The puppies were really barking. Maybe they knew they were being taken away from their mother. They couldn't bark too loud because they were still puppies. Still I heard them barking." "Yes, you are right, it is really possible," the villagers said.

So in every lie you can also find a little bit of truth. Without truth not even a lie can survive. I am telling you that even to lie completely is not possible. This is what Mahavira refers to when he speaks of the multiplicity of truth. If you want to live lovingly and compassionately, you must know these principles. Never insist on anything, just say, "Yes, you are right too." By your own point of view, you can be right too. Do not insist on saying this is black, because you do not know if the other side is white. You can say, according to your point of view, that it is black, but yes, you may be right too. Somehow everybody is right according to his or her point of view, but we must listen to the other side too. You must learn to respect everyone's perspective. Mahavira pointed out the fact that truth has many perspectives, and gave us the seven steps to analyze them. It is a big mathematical principle which helps you to analyze anything and come up with a much clearer perspective of the truth.

Let me give you an example. One day I was in Punjab, in a city called Roper. A doctor came to me and asked if I could suggest to him in one step how he could mathematically find God. I told him to first tell me about himself. "Who are you?" I asked. "I am a surgeon," he said. At that time I was maybe eighteen years old. "Yes, I can tell you mathematically, and in one line, how to find God." So I told him to listen carefully. I said, "Soul (meaning that which knows things and which feels pain, sorrow, happiness, ecstasy and bliss) or light plus matter or karma (karma is also matter) equals *Jiva Atma*. Soul plus matter equals Jiva Atma. Jiva means "living being," so Jiva Atma means "Soul with the body." "Yes, I understand this formula, and it is a good formula," he said. "But how do I realize myself?" he asked. I told him, "Alright, let me tell you how to realize yourself, although for this you must go a little further. Soul minus matter or karma equals *parmatman*. This is what you need to work on," I told him.

What is the difference between God and us? God is light and this light always shines. But we have clouds, karma all around us, and we cannot shine. So soul minus matter or karma becomes God. He understood, and maybe you understand it too. But do you really understand it? I tell you, if you really understand this principle you might suddenly find yourself to be very close to God.

Mahavira gave many formulas like this one. I cannot tell you in one day all of the different principles, but everything he wrote is very beautiful. His teachings are collected in many different books called Agama. Agama means "the treasure of knowledge," and this is what he left us. His teachings are collected in almost forty-five volumes, plus eighty-four extra volumes of commentary.

Today I wanted to highlight his life in celebration of his birthday. He was raised as a prince, he married and had one daughter, but at the age of thirty he left everything behind, went to the jungle and he devoted his whole life to spiritual practice. Twelve years later he achieved enlightenment and shared his light with everyone around him. When a person is so full of light, he or she cannot resist sharing it with the whole universe. It has to be given back. His main principles are *ahimsa* (non-violence) *anekantvad* (the multiplicity of truth) and the seven steps to analyze it.

LEELA: FLOW WITH NATURE

This world is very mysterious and everything we think, feel or do also seems to be a mystery. In Hindu mythology, this mystery is called *leela*. Leela means play, it means game, it means illusion, it means drama, it means projection of mind. Leela means dramatization of every aspect of life including the whole universe, even God itself.

In India it is customary to have lots of plays and dramas. In fact you will hear people say *Krishan Leela* or *Ram Leela* to describe the message of Krishna or the message of Rama. Even though leela is used to describe the drama of life, it is also used to describe much more than that. Many other things are covered when we use the word leela. Everything that happens around us is leela. Whether it is raining or if it is sunny, this is referred to as the"Leela of God." If there are clouds in the sky, again they will say it is the Leela of God. In the real sense there is no need to worry about anything. If you are breathing, just go on breathing. If you are looking at the birds, just look at them. You have to be like a star; the star is twinkling, so let it twinkle. The sun is shining, so let it shine. Whatever is happening, you do not interfere with the happening. If you are thirsty, you drink. If you are hungry, you eat. And if you can really flow with this universal play, you are automatically flowing with leela.

Krishna goes even a little further to describe leela. He says that if one person is killing another, maybe they have to kill; it might be that there is no other way. Or if one person is saving another, again, there might be no other way. In fact, Krishna says, "You cannot interfere with nature." If the lion is hungry, it will chase after its prey; it will hunt in order to eat. Once when I was in meditation I became like a lion. I felt very strange. I perceived that when the lion was running towards the animal he was wondering why his food was running from him. He could not differentiate between food and the animal that was running from him. He simply saw food. The lion has only one motive in his life, and that is to eat.

So if you ask Krishna what this is, Krishna will say: "This is leela." Whether one person is killing another or one person is saving another or if there is a battle or a war, Krishna says not to interfere. Krishna tried to save lots of people. He knew already that in the Mahabharta –"The Great Battle,"which was even larger than World War II – that people could not be saved. The Mahabarta happened five thousand years ago and many people were killed in it. Krishna was saying that there would be no war, even though he knew it would happen again one day. According to Krishna, it was a play. The Mahabharta was a family battle because family members controlled the army. The problem in the Mahabharta was not only the battle itself, but also the killing that had to happen between family members. A grandson needed to kill his grandfather, but stopped himself in the middle of battlefield. He couldn't do it. He came to Krishna and asked, "How could such action be possible?" Krishna answered by asking another question. "Who kills whom?" Krishna asked. "Any thing happens because this is war." Krishna said, "Look, your grandfather is a great warrior, but he killed your son too. What is wrong with you? Why aren't you killing him? This is a battlefield, and you cannot change it!"

The whole world is like a battlefield for this play to take place. We think we get killed, but in the real sense we never get killed. Our soul is immortal. Our being is immortal. We think that if we save someone we will collect many virtues, *punyas* or good karma. It is but only our illusion that makes us think this way. This is why illusion is not separate from the play. At every given moment the play is the natural aspect of life. You are breathing, you are eating, the flowers blossom, the stars twinkle, rivers are flowing, and this is all natural. You cannot interfere with nature; you can only flow with it. When you flow with it, many positive things can happen in your life.

Marpa, a Tibetan saint, had a disciple. One day his disciple asked him what he was doing. Marpa replied, "Nothing." The disciple could not accept his teacher's answer and said, "You must be doing something." Marpa was simply meditating, and in meditation you don't do anything, you just are. But to just be is not easy.

Meditation teaches us to be. But what you really want is to be everything other than being what you really are, while yoga and meditation teach you to just be. Can you be what you are? I know it is hard because when you close your eyes you see only darkness. It is hard to face the dark when your mind wants to see only light. But naturally when you close your eyes, darkness is the only thing you see. Remember one thing: when you are with yourself, with your being, you are helping the whole universe. In the state of being with yourself you lose all resistance and are flowing with the whole universe.

Where there is resistance, you are not flowing with the play. Where there is resistance or tension, know that you will attract to yourself many problems; you will attract unhappiness and all karmas will rush to you. Non-resistance is the secret. Be like a child at play. A child is always relaxed at all times. Can you be like that? If you can do it, you are flowing with this leela – with this play, with this universe. But if you resist, you will be unable to flow.

Resistance creates all kinds of troubles. So leela means to be relaxed. Are you tense when you are playing? You cannot play if you are tensed. Can you play golf if you are tense? You cannot make even one good shot when you are tense. You hit the ball and the ball will go somewhere other than where you intend for it to go. So you must relax. Where there is relaxation there is no resistance. When you are with yourself many wonderful things can happen to you and you will be a totally different person. You can be a Krishna too.

Krishna accepts everything. This is why in Indian mythology Krishna is considered the full incarnation of God. But Rama resisted. Rama was also God, but he resisted all the time. Rama was always worried about what people thought about him. His wife was kidnapped by a demon that kept her in captivity for six months. How could he take her back? He was worried about being criticized, and this is why he left her. Krishna would not have done it. Krishna would have accepted the fact she had been kidnapped. After all, it was not her mistake. Krishna would say, "Accept what is."

When there is acceptance, it means that you are flowing with the play. Krishna would accept war and he would accept happiness. Krishna would accept anything. You will be surprised to see that Krishna accepted many things, even those things which do not fit in society, and he would say that they were not in his hands. Rukmani, Krishna's wife, before their marriage wrote Krishna a letter saying, "My brother and father both wanted me to marry someone else, but you and I have been part of each other for many lifetimes and I cannot take this chance to lose you. The wedding is being arranged and in few days I will be marrying this other person. If you want me, come and get me and take me away with you." As soon as Krishna received the letter, he told his brother that he would go and bring Rukmani over to his palace. There was no other way. The brother asked if he needed an army to escort him, but Krishna felt it was not necessary, being that Rukmani had already preplanned where to meet. The brother said, "But they have the biggest army and they will be fighting you." Krishna replied, "Do not worry, I don't need any army. I am not kidnapping her; she will be kidnapping me. Actually, many people are in favor of me." So he went ahead with Rukmani's plan.

If you flow with your life without understanding all the dimensions of an issue, you might encounter more problems. But the enlightened person sees all sides. The person who has reached higher consciousness can see all sides and can see if an action will bring more trouble or less trouble. But for you, because you cannot see all sides, you resist and resistance never takes you anywhere.

Try to flow, or at least flow when you have some free time or when you are relaxed. When you walk, flow with your walking. If you go to a tree, flow with it, or look at the flowers in the garden. In those moments you can be with yourself. If you flow even for only a short time, lots of things will change inside of you.

Whatever you are carrying is not yours. Do you think that anger is yours? No, it is an outer thing. Do you think that violence is yours? No, you adopted it from somewhere. But if you love nature, love the stars, and love the flowers, your passion for life will be alive in you. Love, because it belongs to you and because it is yours, will make you dance with the whole of nature. Seek your passion and you will feel much higher. If you try to flow with this universe, the universe will help you. You first need to understand what this play is, what this leela is, and then, meditation will happen. But it will happen later on, after you have learned to flow with nature. Leela, God's leela, is really amazing.

COINCIDENCE

Nothing is unusual in our lives. There is a reason behind everything, but we do not understand what that reason is. We think it is coincidence. This is what Hume was thinking. Hume thought that everything happens by coincidence. Somebody dies; a plane crashes; a car gets into an accident - Hume would immediately say it is coincidence. Even if a baby is born blind, he would still say it is coincidence. It is not coincidence. There is always a reason things happen, and you need to know what it is.

Let me give you an example. In India, I knew of one small village in which all babies born could not survive more than two years. It was happening for years. Was it coincidence? I knew of another village in which babies would survive eight years and then die. Out of ten babies, only two would live beyond the age of eight. Is it coincidence or is it something else? This concept is not easily understood.

You have to go deep inside and you will be surprised to see what you discover. At some point you will start communicating with animals, with trees, and with birds. You will be surprised because you can even feel you have become them. One day, in meditation, I suddenly communicated with a lion. I felt like a lion and was among the lions. I was in the jungle and could see a lion running after an animal. To you it might appear unusual seeing a lion running after another animal, killing for his food. But the lion does not think this way. When I had that communication I felt that the lion did not think he was killing. I was also shocked to understand what the lion was feeling. The lion did not think he was killing, he felt that his food was running from him. "This is my food - why is it running from me? Why do I have to run after my food?" the lion thought. We see it as an animal, but the lion sees the running animal as his food and wonders why his food is slipping away from him.

When you communicate with other lives, you will be shocked to find that many things happening to you have a reason behind them. Unless you realize this, you cannot know reality. Try to communicate, try to be a tree and realize how the tree really feels if someone climbs it. Yes, the tree is happy when you trim all its dried branches. You become very happy too after trimming your nails or your hair. But if you destroy a branch, which is not yet dry, do you think the tree is happy? Yes, trimming dried branches makes the tree feel relieved, but to destroy a branch that is still alive hurts the tree.

There is a reason behind every occurrence. It is not coincidence. Scientists will give you reasons to determine why something happens. They will blame DNA. They will have many reasons. But are all of their reasons reasonable? Life is not one-dimensional. Life does not work one way. There are several reasons why things happen the way they do. Maybe that soul which is about to take birth wants to be blind because this is not his or her first life. When people find themselves in certain situations, they might refuse to see anything and choose to be born blind. This is one reason why a baby can be born blind. You will be shocked to hear of this one real

106

incident. A young girl fell in love with a boy. It was her first love. However, her parents did not accept the boy. They told her that she could never see him ever again. Do you know what happened to her? After being prohibited to see him, she lost her vision. I talked to her personally and she expressed her thoughts to me. She said, "If I cannot see the person whom I love so deeply, then everything in life is useless." These exact words went so deep into her heart that she lost her vision. Her parents, before coming to me, took her to every healer possible. They took her to monks, they took her to doctors, but nothing helped her. Doctors could not find anything wrong with her eyes. They could not find any physiological problem and everything was in order. The fact that she could not see was a mystery to them.

When the intention goes deep, the mind cooperates. In her case, the mind felt it was worthless to see. It is not coincidence that a baby is born blind. In a person's past life, before dying, that person could have made a wish not to see in their next life. Maybe they saw too much suffering and wished to be born blind. Sometimes scientific reasons are not enough. Something else is at work. As in the case of this particular girl, her parents took her here and there, from one doctor to another doctor, from one monk to another monk, to be healed. They tried for more than a year when they finally met me. I suggested a few things to them and I asked if their intention was really in favor of her regaining her vision. "Of course, this is our reason for coming to you," they said. I suggested they bring the boy she loved so much to see her. It might be that by hearing his voice her mind would respond favorably. They listened to my suggestion and they followed my advice. They brought the boy and sure enough, as soon as she heard his voice, she got her vision back.

There are many reasons behind situations which determine the outcome of the situation. The law of karma is very difficult to understand. But if you understand even a little bit you might be really surprised to see how it works. Nothing is coincidental, as Hume would like you to think. There is always a reason behind everything that happens. In 2000, one hundred and eighteen people died due to the failure of the Kursk, a Russian submarine. According to the law of karma, those one hundred and eighteen deaths may have possibly saved the whole world. If this had not happened, perhaps that submarine would have exploded. The outcome could have been disastrous.

We only see one side of things, and are unable to see the other side. Take Saddam Hussein, for example. We see him as a very bad man, a devil, but we do not see the other side. We don't know what would have happened if he had not invaded Kuwait. We see just one reason. We see that he is a bad man, the devil. We are only attuned to what is visible, and are unable to see the other side. If he had not occupied Kuwait, how do we know that many more people would not have died? Also with Hitler: if he had not killed the Jews, do we know what the outcome would have been? Or vice versa. We know that what he did was very bad. He was not supposed to do it and I am not supporting or in favor of either Hitler's or Hussein's actions. They were bad and violent men. But we do not see the other side. If they had not done those things, what would have happened? Maybe, instead of thousands of people getting killed, millions would have gotten killed. We do not know the consequences of a different decision. Gandhi is another example. His actions were very good, while their outcome was disastrous. He tried to save India by non-violence and he tried very hard not to kill any English people. He wanted them to live peacefully. He sent a message to the whole nation not to react to British cruelties. India never retaliated, even though her people were being beaten and tortured. Gandhi could see only one side. He never saw the other side until it was too late. Because the people of India became so non-violent, the British divided the country in two. One side became Pakistan. It was during the partition that Gandhi's heart was broken. He cried after seeing the results. He never thought the consequence would be so violent. A million people were killed because of this partition. He saved one hundred thousand people, but the result of his actions killed one million people. Hindus and Muslims were killing each other right and left. His message of non-violence was persuasive enough to convince the nation not to react to the British, but it never penetrated their hearts. It remained suppressed and once the time became favorable, it exploded. It is easy to comment on what we see, but to know the other side is very difficult.

We only see one side; we do not see the other side. The other side is hidden. This is why we are so confused. We think it is coincidence, but if you go deeper you will be surprised to see that nothing is without a reason. Every thing that happens has its reason. The birds chirping, the flowers blossoming, the stars shinning, they all have a reason hidden behind what is obvious to us. Why are the stars shining? Why? Nobody knows. You are alive, but you do not know why you are alive. You only know that you are alive. But why don't you know the reason? By working on lifting yourself higher you will come to know what is the reason working behind you being alive. Nothing is coincidence; all is cause and effect. Light a fire, put a pot of water on it, and the water starts boiling. Put the water into the freezer and it gets icy. The theory of cause and effect needs to really be understood. Nothing is coincidence. Just yesterday, while having breakfast, Daniela asked me, "Did Eileen call you?" Not even two seconds after she asked the question the phone rang, and it was Eileen calling.

Maybe she was feeling it deep down.

We think it is coincidence. No, it is not coincidence. It is some kind of power working inside of you, and you are not in touch with it. Can you imagine what it would be like if you were in touch with this power? If you are always in touch with this power you can see millions of stars, and the mystery will not be a mystery anymore. Elevate yourself to a higher state of consciousness. Lift yourself higher as much as possible and coincidence will disappear from your mind.

GOD IS WATCHING

There was a king who had three grown sons. All three lived very lavish lifestyles, and none of them turned out to be worthy of the throne. The king was confused which one of the three princes was to become his successor. Was it to be the oldest, the middle one, or the youngest? Being that the king was a very frustrated person, he had to find how to choose the right one to be his successor.

One day he summoned his three sons. He gave each one a bird and he suggested to them to "Go to a place where no one is watching you, then kill the little bird and bring it back to me." "What kind of stupidity is this?" thought the oldest son. "I will simply go behind the wall and kill the bird." So he did. The middle son thought, "Maybe someone is watching me here by the wall. I had better go a little further into the garden where there are lots of trees. There I will hide between the trees, and when I see that no one is watching me, I will kill the bird." After their task was done, both sons came back to the king. The youngest son, however, decided to go further away. He did not choose to go behind the wall like the oldest brother, or into the forest like the middle brother. He thought it was possible to be watched there. So he went elsewhere instead. He went very deep into the forest, where the trees were the thickest. But he could feel he was being watched there too. "Any bird on the tree could see me," he thought. So he decided to go by the bank of the river. He looked all around and saw that no one was there. "Well, no one is here, so maybe this is the best place to kill this little bird." He was ready to kill it when he suddenly saw a reflection in the water. He looked at it and saw that it was a flock of birds flying overhead. "Even here I can be seen - these flying birds are watching me." Finally, the birds passed and he felt it to be the right time to complete his task. So he tried once again to kill the bird, but he found that he couldn't. He was puzzled and thought, "No one is here; no humans; no birds and no animals - why am I unable to kill this little bird?" He thought about it a lot and saw that it was God who was watching him. "I know that God is everywhere and that he is omnipresent, so God must be watching me. I cannot kill this little bird now. But if I don't kill the bird, I will be disobeying my father. Still, not even this can make me do it." So he didn't, and he took the bird back to his father instead.

In the Sufi religion, "God is watching" is a device which has been used for centuries with anyone who wants to learn to meditate or to improve oneself. To be aware that "God is watching" all of our actions, thoughts and feelings, either while we are awake, asleep or dreaming, is a way to develop awareness and purity. This approach really works. If you try it you will see that being constantly aware that God is watching you makes it impossible to have bad thoughts or indulge in any lower qualities. When you know that God is watching you, no lower qualities can contaminate or touch your consciousness. Hypothetically speaking, "God is watching" is the device from which awareness is awakened. When awareness blossoms, all of your bad thoughts and lower qualities – or negativities such as jealousy, pride, violence, etc. – will completely disappear.

This is exactly what that youngest prince experienced. He became aware and saw that there was no place to hide. He knew that even if people or animals were not there to see his action, God would be there to witness it. This is why he couldn't kill the little bird and chose to disobey the king's command instead. He was disappointed to disobey his father, but he felt he had no other choice and he returned home with the bird still alive.

The prince came back and apologized to the king for not being able to execute his wish. The King responded by saying, "Look, your eldest brothers could kill the bird, why couldn't you do it?" The youngest son replied, "I went few places but somehow I was always watched. I went as far as the river, but still, someone was there. I could not do it. Forgive me father, but I could not kill this bird because I couldn't find a place where no one was watching me, because God was always watching me. Father, even though you may think I have disobeyed you, I do not want your kingdom and I do not want your riches. I could not kill this little bird. God was watching me the whole time, so where could I have gone to kill it?" His response was the reason why the king selected him. He wanted the best successor and he got it.

If you can keep this awareness and know moment to moment that God is watching you, do you think you can have bad thoughts, have anger, have jealousy or any of the nonsense you are doing? If you are aware, even when you eat one piece of bread, maybe you can be thankful to God. Because of that piece of bread you have life, you have breath, and two eyes to look at it. The Sufis say, "Be aware that God is watching you, always watching you." This is the best advice, and the only device that works. It will enlighten you and you will become a totally different person. Such a device can bring you total transformation, but it cannot be a momentary event. The awareness that "God is watching" has to be constantly inside of you. The secret and the alchemy of transformation is hidden it these words: "God is watching."

DIWALI

In Indian culture, *Diwali* is a very important festival, just as Christmas is in the West. Diwali (or Dipavali or Dipmala) is known as the Festival of Lights and means the row of candles or row of *dipak*. Dipak is a little clay pot with a wick in which you put a little oil, and then you light it.

Diwali has been celebrated in India for centuries. Historically, we do not know when it started. However, for Hindus, Diwali represents Lord Rama's victory of good over evil. Lord Rama, who at that time had been in exile, was living with his wife Sita and his brother in the forest. One day Rama discovered that Ravna, the evil demon king, had kidnapped his wife. Once Rama and his brother found out she had been kidnapped they decided to go all the way to Lanka looking for her. However, to get there Rama had to build a long bridge over the ocean. It was not an easy task, but he managed to build it somehow. Everyone helped, even the little birds and squirrels. Everyone wanted him to cross the ocean and get to Lanka. Finally Rama crossed the ocean and reached Lanka. There he fought the demon and won the battle. Once Sita was liberated, together they went back to Ayodhya, the holy city, where people enthusiastically welcomed them, especially Rama. The night was completely dark and in order to celebrate their return, the people lit many dipakas and with them they decorated the whole city. From this, Diwali evolved.

In the mainstream of Indian culture, Diwali represents the victory of good over evil; however, the Jains (who are also part of the same tradition) have a different point of view. For them, Diwali is significant because of Lord Mahavira. Lord Mahavira was born in 599 BC and taught for several years, and all of his teachings have been collected in many volumes called *Agamas*.

At the age of thirty, Mahavira left his home and began to do many spiritual practices, by which later on he became enlightened. After his enlightenment he went on to spread the teachings of non-violence, truthfulness, non-stealing and non-possession. He kept on teaching them for the next thirty years, until the time he left his body. These principles are very important and if you fully understand even one of them, your life will be totally changed. Even one principle - fully understood - is enough for all of the others to automatically follow.

Mahavira kept on lecturing until the end of his life. In fact, his last lecture went on for three consecutive days. He knew, as everyone else knew, that his time had come. Still, he kept on lecturing. Eighteen kings came and sat in front of him with their subjects. Continuously listening to his last sermons for the whole three days, none of them ate or moved from their places. They remained present with him until he took his last breath, then he merged with God and achieved nirvana.

It was midnight when Mahavira achieved nirvana. The night was very dark and became even darker once Mahavira had left his body. People became upset because his light was gone. So the kings took out all of their jewels, and the jewels created a great light. Symbolically, the kings wanted to recreate the light which was no longer with them. They felt that if one light had disappeared, they would recreate another, shining everywhere.

Before his nirvana, Mahavira decided it was time for Gautama, his chief disciple, to leave his side. Gautama was always with him and followed him just like a shadow. Gautama was far too attached to his master. For this reason, Mahavira felt that unless he sent him away, Gautama would never achieve enlightenment. So one day he told Gautama to go to a different town to teach the people there. Gautama, who could never refuse Mahavira's orders, departed for the other town. Later on, when Gautama heard that Mahavira had achieved nirvana, he began to weep just like a baby. He could not understand why Mahavira had sent him away. He was so distraught that he couldn't stop crying. Everyone tried to console him. They tried to tell him that this body is temporary, and that one day we all have to go and leave it behind. Gautama knew it intellectually, but this understanding had yet to penetrate the depth of his heart. Still, he could not stop his crying. But as people kept consoling him, all of a sudden their words penetrated deeply into his being. He became settled, and his attachment to Mahavira disappeared. And on the same night that Mahavira achieved nirvana, Gautama achieved enlightenment. As one light merged with God, another was lit.

Actually, whether you follow the Hindu or the Jain point of view, the real meaning of Diwali remains the same: "You must light your heart." By destroying the darkness, ignorance will be gone and once your ignorance is destroyed, automatically your heart will be lit. This is what Diwali really means. Diwali represents victory of good over evil. We must always look at ourselves and recognize what goes on inside. Besides looking at all of the good in us, we must also be able to see all of the evil things and negative thoughts that go on inside.

Within Diwali you can find other aspects of the tradition, one of which is to call upon *Lakshmi*, the Goddess of wealth and prosperity. Lakshmi, who never moves away from God, on Diwali Night leaves Vishnu's side and roams around the whole world and when midnight strikes she enters any home to which she has been called upon. But her conditions are that the house has to be fully cleaned, fully lighted, and that the people are still awake. People prepare for her coming. They fill a big golden or silver dish with a little dipak in the center and with flowers, fruits and desserts all around it as an offering to the Goddess. When the Goddess comes, she will not eat the offerings; she will only take their fragrance.

Let me tell you a little secret. You might not be aware of it, but all of these angels and Goddesses are within us and they live among us. But how can we really be aware of them and know them? On the next Diwali night, you can prepare a beautiful bowl with flowers and fruits and a little dipak in the center as an offering to the Goddess and to the angels. Later on, if you notice that the fragrance is gone, it means that the Goddess had accepted your offering. If you see this sign it means that your future days are going to be very lucky. Try it and find out for yourself. But be aware, because with any good tradition you can find bad traditions too. Actually, the whole world is a combination of good and bad. Take the Tantric tradition for example. On Diwali Night they also perform some special *sadhana* or spiritual practices. However, the intent is not to attract the Goddess, but bad spirits. They do their rituals for negative purposes, and offer wine to attract the bad spirits so that the bad spirits will harm others.

But if you do it, do it to invite the Goddess of wealth. For this you have to do lots of cleaning and cleansing. You know that all of this evil does reside in you, so to invite the Goddess, you must clean and clear yourself of it. After cleansing, prepare a big pot with a dipak in the center, with some flowers and different fragrances displayed around it. Then recite the Mahalakshmi mantra:

AUM HRIM SHRIM KAMALE KAMALALAYE PRASEED PRASEED HRIM SHRIM HRIM AUM MAHALAKSHMYIE NAMAH

You cannot escape it; both good and evil reside in you and all around you. A painter, after having made many paintings, felt he would not be fully satisfied unless he could make another masterpiece in which he could capture divinity in the eyes of a person. He went everywhere to find that person, but he had hard time finding the right one. After crossing fields and mountains, he finally came across a shepherd boy. He was fully taken by such eyes and amazed that he had finally come across divinity. He asked the shepherd boy if he could paint his portrait. So he did, and the result was incredible. He had created a real masterpiece.

Years passed, and the painter was old. Still, another desire was lingering in him; he wanted to paint the opposite of divinity. As he had once captured divinity, now he wanted to capture the look of Satan in the eyes of someone else. Again he started searching, going to every prison in hope to find such a person. He visited mental hospitals where people were delusional. Finally, he saw a man in a prison that looked to him like the devil, and he painted his portrait. Then, after he was done with the painting, he decided to show the evil looking man the portrait of the shepherd boy that he had painted years before. "I made two masterpieces in my life, and here they are," he told the evil-looking man. "In one I have captured divinity, and in the other I have captured evil." Even the painter was amazed by his ability to capture these two extremes. The evil-looking man started crying. "Why do you cry?" the painter asked. The man replied, "The person in this painting which portrays divinity is also me. Don't you recognize me? I am the same shepherd boy you once painted, but things went wrong for me and I committed a crime, which is why I am in this prison today. But I am the same person."

So both divinity and evil are inside of you. Both possibilities are inside each individual, but they have to be searched for. Actually, if by searching you discover these two dimensions, you can then become a totally different person. And so, victory over evil is about conquering your mind, conquering your thoughts - negative thoughts. When you can do this it means that Diwali has become a continuous celebration.

To the average Indian, these are merely rituals to bring the people together socially. But to the spiritually inclined person, these rituals can be used as a way to understand the Self, and to be aware of the real truth permeating the whole universe. So the real meaning of Diwali is to become *swasth*, meaning "staying fully with your Self." When everything around you and in you is cleansed and pure, you will be swasth. All these rituals symbolize stillness. If you want to be enlightened you must stay still from everything. Still from your mind, still from your anger, still from all of your emotions, and one day, you will be enlightened. All the lights that are used on Diwali are symbolic for stillness. But if you can really become still, real light can happen inside of you.

This is Diwali, and Diwali means "light your heart." This day is a very spiritual day. It is said that praying or reciting mantras for an entire year will not yield as many results as if you pray or recite mantras on Diwali Night. The results are a thousand times greater.

You must work on it now, while you have the chance. Don't think that once you leave this body your life ends. You are wrong! The body can only be recycled and it will continue being recycled until you achieve enlightenment. You have to achieve enlightenment because enlightenment is everything.

In the alchemy of transformation lies enlightenment, just as in the alchemy of transforming iron lies gold. To become enlightened, the process is like turning iron into gold, and once you have become gold you cannot fall back into being iron again. Enlightenment means that you have merged with God, like Mahavira did when he achieved nirvana. You can change iron into gold, but you can never change gold into iron. It is impossible, even if you put it in the fire. Gold cannot be recycled or destroyed. You can make it purer and purer, but you can never change its properties. The more you put yourself in the fire of spiritual practices, the purer you become. Make it your goal to become the purest gold. This is the goal of Diwali, which symbolically means "light your heart." Light your heart and you will see your real beauty. I wish from the depth of my being that your heart will be lit today. Repeat mantras, chant the universal sounds of AUM and you will reap great results.

NON-VIOLENCE

Non-violence is a vast concept and it encompasses many different things.

Not killing or not hurting doesn't make a person non-violent. Using a weapon to kill is not necessarily the only way to kill. Maybe your thoughts, mind, and emotions, or maybe your way of helping and hurting kills someone all the time.

Someone wrote, "If you want to kill truth you don't have to use any swords or weapons. You just have to hail the truth. Make a slogan and loudly say – 'Hail, Hail to the truth!' - and this is a sure way to kill it." But I am telling you that to hail to anything is a violent act.

Ignorance is the main cause of all kinds of killing, and the main reason which keeps people away from understanding the real meaning of non-violence. Praise can be poisonous if you do not have right understanding. Furthermore, if you have a lack of true knowledge, even your good deeds can be poisonous. Let's take truth as an example; as soon as you speak about truth, you have already killed it. Moreover, once you have killed it, you have also killed the possibility to know God.

Truth does not need you to speak loudly. Truth comes from your heart. It is a heart phenomenon. It does not even need to be spoken. Truth does not need to be told. Truth can be realized, truth can be experienced, but it cannot be told. This is the reason why people have difficulty realizing God.

God is truth itself. So if truth cannot be told, and if God is truth, how can God be told? Many people will say, "Oh, we talk to God!" But when I ask them what God looks like they will give different descriptions. Some will say God is a man. Again I ask, "How do you know that God is a man? How can you be sure that God is not a female or an animal's shape?" They do not know, and this is why they cannot answer my question.

I think people go too much into imagination. Instead of realizing truth, they would rather dream of it. But if God is realized, it will be a totally different experience. God has no face, no form or shape. God just shines, and this shining spreads everywhere.

In Japan, if you go to a Zen teacher or guru, he or she will tell you that if you really want to find the truth, to find God you must first find your original face. The face you had even before you were born. Can you see your real face? People sit in meditation trying everything in order to find how they looked before they were born. But it is very difficult to find that face. Nonetheless, if somebody finds it they can find God too.

I am telling you, God is hidden inside of you. It just needs to be revealed. You don't have to go to Mount Everest to find it. You don't have to go to any temple or synagogue or to any church to find God. Even the Bible says that God is everywhere and that God is omnipotent and omnipresent.

God is everywhere, but you haven't yet learned to respect each and every living being. So if God is everywhere, why don't we respect everything, even non-living beings?

Let me give you an example. When I was in Delhi one fellow called me and wanted to ask me a question. I told him to come and visit me. When the fellow came, people were sitting with me. He opened the door, he took his shoes off, came in and sat in front of me. From the moment he opened the door and entered I watched each one of his actions and when the right moment came, I pointed out to him what I had observed.

I noticed that he opened the door in an angry way. I also noticed that the way he took off his shoes had lots of anger. So the very first thing I asked him was to go to the door and apologize and ask for its forgiveness. He shook his head in amazement. I repeated myself and said, "Yes, go to the door and apologize and ask for forgiveness, and after that go to your shoes and ask for their forgiveness too. If you really want to ask me any questions first do as you are told."

He really had a hard time following my instructions, but he had to. He went to the door and without any feelings he said, "I am sorry." "Not like that," I interjected. Your apologies must come form your heart. You must feel that you are really sorry to have hurt them. You opened the door and you took off your shoes with such anger, and that showed me that you don't respect things."

Where there is no respect it shows that you don't know God yet; you don't know truth yet. It shows there is violence in your behavior. And where there is violence there is no truth; there is no God. If you don't know how to respect things, how can you respect other living beings, or as a matter of fact, *God*?

It is best that you first learn from your home. That's why there's the saying "Charity begins at home." Learn from home; learn from your parents. If you can respect your parents and if you can respect your children, maybe you will learn, and you will eventually come to know yourself and God too.

When there is no respect there is violence, and where there is violence there is no truth, and where there is no truth there is no God. To know truth or to know God, you must learn what non-violence is.

In Sanskrit it is called *ahimsa* which means not killing and not hurting. ahimsa is the non-doing approach. Ahimsa approaches truth through negation. This is the reason why people have a hard time digesting it. On the other end, love adopts the positive approach, which works perfectly in society. No wonder Jesus became so popular as the messenger of ahimsa. Lord Mahavira is barely known in history even though ahimsa is the ultimate principle to connect you to the Supreme.

Ahimsa simply means oneness with all living beings. It means you are really connected to the whole. Ahimsa is like a zero and like nothingness, while love is like one. Love is visible while non-violence is invisible. Ahimsa is not separate from you. It is you. It is just like your bones, your muscles, your pores or your blood. While love seems to be more on the surface, ahimsa goes even deeper. Love needs to be told. Ahimsa goes on in silence, and in this silence many things, many possibilities, can occur. Ahimsa does not need to be hailed; this is why it cannot be killed. But love needs expressions, it needs gestures, and it needs to be spoken loudly. This is why people have failed in love and become victorious in non-violence.

Actually, non-violence is the by-product of realizing truth. To understand this principle is to understand how violent you are even in your good intentions.

Many times you have found yourself in situations in which you tried to make another person happy. You had good intentions, but that person was not ready to take that much happiness and felt violated. Your good intentions were forced on another and if you force anything you have automatically put yourself in a situation whereby violence is the result. Your kindness creates antagonism between you and that person and consequently you feel rejected.

It is very difficult to capture the subtleties of this statement and see how good intentions can turn into violent acts. You cannot make people happy by forcing your desires on them. If you try, you will be rejected.

Psychologically speaking, I will tell you (and I know I am not wrong) it is not certain that a rich person's son or a good person's son will turn out to be rich or good. Exceptions are there. On the other end, the opposite can be also true. A poor parent or a bad parent's sons can be rich and very good. The possibilities are there. However, when very good parents try to teach their child to be very good, that goodness might backfire on the parents. The child may rebel by going against parental instructions because goodness becomes too heavy on the child and consequently the child cannot take it.

If good parents want to reach their children and teach them to be good, they have to be diplomatic, otherwise they will encounter difficulties. Children get bored with too much goodness and run in the opposite direction.

Henry Ford, a wealthy person, once went to Europe. When he came to his hotel, he requested the cheapest room. The concierge recognized him and offered a very expensive room instead and said to him, "If I am not mistaken, you are Henry Ford. Why do you want such an inexpensive room? When your children come they request the most expensive room." Henry Ford answered, "They are Henry Ford's children and they deserve to stay in the most expensive room because they are a rich father's children. But I do not forget my childhood; I am a poor father's child and need the least expensive room." It means that by remembering his origins, Henry Ford did not want to feed his ego. He accepted his riches for his children, but for himself chose to live like a poor man.

If good parents try too hard to make their children good, they might get rejected. They might have to use diplomacy or take them to a teacher who can give the right guidance, and maybe then they will learn something good.

The opposite can also happen. If children see that their parents are not good, they might do the contrary and can turn out very good. I have seen many examples of this.

India's Prime Minister Lal Bahadur Shastri was born in a very poor family. They were so poor that Shastri had to swim every morning across the river Ganges to go to school because he didn't have enough money to take the ferry. He struggled a lot, but look at him. He became the Prime Minister of India and was loved by everyone.

I think children need right direction, but without too much force. Sometimes a good parent's weakness is to insist too much for their children to be good. When they force it too much, children find it difficult to follow, so they rebel. Parents need to understand that they need to give guidelines without forcing them. Just let them be happy and enjoy where they are and allow them to learn by example rather than force.

If you cannot give your children right direction, bring them to a teacher who knows and who can understand them. Children are very receptive and might learn faster than you could ever imagine. Right guidance is the best gift you can ever give to your children. With right guidance they can turn out to be very good and balanced people in society.

This teaching follows the same guidelines as non-violence does. It is very difficult and very rarely understood. People force it too much and they give no space for learning to happen. Parents are unable to give them right guidance because of their lack of right understanding.

What the majority of people understand by non-violence is not killing and not hurting. But to really understand non-violence is to understand truth; it is to understand God. However, people are more willing to hail the truth rather than to realize it.

If someone is hurt and needs help, under the notion of non-violence, what would be the right form of action? A non-violent person might totally pass it by. Still, in his passing there could be lots of compassion. Let me give you an example and you might understand what I mean.

An angel appeared in front of a Sufi saint and said, "God is very happy with you. Demand anything and your wish will be fulfilled." The saint smiled and said, "If God is happy with me, what else do I need? I do not need anything else, that's enough." "No," the angel replied, "wish for something. You must wish for something." "I cannot wish is my best wish," the saint said. "God is happy and that's enough for me." The angel did not give up, and said, "Okay, if you don't want to wish from God, I am also happy with you, so wish from me. I want to give you my blessings before I leave. I want to give you that kind of blessing by which everything will blossom and by which even the sick will be healed, and if you touch a dead tree or a dead animal their life will be regained. Anywhere you go, whatever you touch will be totally different." The saint interrupted the angel and said, "Wait a moment, don't grant this wish to me. Grant to my shadow that whatever it touches will be healed, be it a dead tree or a sick person." "*Tathastu* (fulfilled)," the angel said.

The saint walked everywhere, healing thousands and thousands of people, never knowing what he did. Wherever he passed and his shadow touched something, all and everything was healed. He had no conscious awareness of what was happening and did not want his ego to take credit for any of it.

Truth does not need you to speak loudly. Truth comes from your heart. To understand this is to be non-violent. Healing occurs merely by your passing, and all flowers blossom. To fully understand and follow the principle of non-violence brings you to the truth. Through this process, the being and the aura expands, bringing about lots of good and lots of healing, and it will help anyone who comes near. The person, however, is unaware of all the good that is happening. It is not him that is doing the good, but his expansion. This is what non-violence is.

I remembered hearing that in Madhya Pradesh there was a Magga Baba. People used to steal him. Can you imagine people stealing a monk? It was believed that wherever he went, everything changed. If he went to someone's house, everything changed; if he went into town, the town became prosperous. People would come in the middle of the night while he was asleep and they would take his bed, with him on it, and he never objected. No matter where they took him, he did not resist; he always allowed himself to be taken. People were crazy about him and there was nothing they would not do for him. They would massage his feet and his legs, they were so taken by him.

This really happened – it is not a story. It happened in central India, and not even too far back in history. It happened about forty years ago. Wherever he went he created miracles, lots of healing, abundance and happiness. If you really learn non-violence, you can achieve that state of consciousness which can really heal people and everything you come in contact with. But in order to achieve it you have to go beyond both *sukha* (happiness and joy), and *dukha* (unhappiness and sorrow).

Going beyond pain is very easy, but going beyond happiness is very difficult. No one wants pain, but everyone wants happiness. However, you must be very careful because in giving happiness you could very easily inflict lots of pain too. To the average observer this information is not correct, but a person who has achieved deeper understanding will see that it is true.

Have you ever thought that by giving happiness you might create unhappiness? To see it you have to be very observant. This is why non-violence is a very big concept. You cannot force a person to change because by trying to change a person you are unknowingly inflicting pain. You cannot do this. The only thing you can do is to flow and fulfill yourself fully.

When you are fulfilled and your aura has expanded, there is no need for any advertisement. Flowers do not say, "We have blossomed." Whoever comes near will recognize the beauty. That's what happens when you become non-violent. You have transformed and blossomed. You have fulfilled your life and filled yourself with that kind of light which affects anyone who comes near it. In your blossoming you have become non-violent.

Merely saving a little goat or a little fly does not make you non-violent. By saving a life you think you have done something good and you will go to heaven. This kind of saving is usually motivated by your fears or desires. Non-violence is not about doing. Doing has motivation connected to it. Non-violence is about being, about blossoming, and about non-doing. So when you have blossomed, your presence changes and everything around you is saved. So there is no need to save. So what you need to do is to make yourself perfect. Can you do that? So by changing yourself, you can change others. This is what you need to do. Only if you are lit you can light another. Light yourself with non-violence.

In India, Gandhi and Subhas Chandra Bose are considered to be very non-violent. But people who understand non-violence have the wrong notion of it. Their understanding can be compared to a beggar who comes to a house. A child is standing there looking at the beggar begging. The compassionate father gives $100 to the beggar. The child, not understanding the value of money, goes from neighbor to neighbor criticizing his father for being so stingy, for being a miser who cannot even give a penny to the beggar but only a piece of paper. The beggar needed food, or money to buy food, but his father gave him a piece of paper instead of giving him a few pennies. The child, not understanding the value of paper currency, criticized the father even though the father gave lots more than just a few pennies.

So Gandhi's understanding of non-violence was like a child who can only understand the value of pennies. And people, not knowing the difference, respect Gandhi a lot. But do you know who the real non-violent one was? I will tell you. There was one fellow, his name was Aurobindo, and he was once very active in politics, but he suddenly left politics and never came back. But in history there is not even one word on him. No mentioning of Aurobindo's name as the one who helped India to become free. Yes, Gandhi is mentioned, or Subhas Chandra Bose or other leaders, but not Aurobindo.

Shri Aurobindo left politics and started expanding his aura instead, and it became so vast that wherever he lived people were changed and became non-violent. Wherever Aurobindo was present there was no violence. Actually, all the violence happened in the north, in Pakistan. But where Aurobindo was there was no violence at all. Aurobindo changed the person quietly (like Gandhi was changed, like Subhas Chandra Bose was changed, and like all the other leaders were changed) in his silence, but his name is not mentioned in history.

I am telling you that if we could perceive the aura of the person we would know who is really non-violent. Even though we have Kirlian photography we still cannot perceive the human aura. In the future, scientists might find the way and history would be changed. Then Gandhi will be recognized as the child who did not know the difference between pennies and paper money, and Aurobindo would be recognized for who he really was. He would be recognized for the perfect person who taught non-violence while remaining silent. This is what non-violence means.

If you too can expand your aura, everywhere you go everything will change, everything will blossom and everything will prosper. The flowers will start blossoming, dead trees will turn green, the sick will be healed, with no need to speak anymore. Truth and God will speak for you, and you will be a fully non-violent person.

If a person expands this energy or aura, a lion will not attack a bull or a goat while in their presence. A snake will not attack a mouse, and a mongoose will forget his enmity towards the snake. In that person's presence, all of this is bound to happen. It is a miracle. It is ahimsa. It is non-violence. It is truth and it is God.

UNIVERSE IS A PLAY

When I say that this universe is a play I mean we have to participate in it as if we participating in a play. We must be like the actor who plays his part. When I say you must participate in the part it means you have to constantly change your masks in accordance with the role you are playing. When a mother is with her children she plays the role of a mother, wearing the mask of a mother. But as soon as her husband comes home, her mask changes. She uses different masks at different times, and with different people. When dealing with her children she wears the mask of the mother. When dealing with her husband she wears the mask of the wife. When dealing with her sister she wears the mask of the sister, etc. This is how the mask changes.

We go on changing our masks our whole life, identifying only with them, sticking with them, never attempting to go beyond them. This is the reason why we do not progress spiritually. We constantly change our masks, and this constant changing of masks keeps us from reaching the ultimate goal.

Not only can we not reach our goals, we become habitual to these changing of masks. We can't even think of looking at anything else. We are such experts at this. We can change our mask so rapidly that we are not even aware we are doing it. We really are great actresses and actors. We daily play out our own dramas, unaware of how destructive this game is and unaware of how many problems it creates for us. We think this is a great thing that we are doing. We do not know that this play is hurting us and it is deferring our growth. It does not take us anywhere. This is why I suggest for you to be a witness. It is simply a role you are playing and the role is not you. Accept the play and the different roles you have to play. If you accept your role-playing, soon the witnessing aspect will take over and you will be able to play the role without any involvement. Once you are aware that it is a play, you will heighten the possibility for growth.

Remember and know that the play is merely a drama, not reality. A play emulates the situation of the facts. It depicts reality, but it is not reality. Take a movie for example: it depicts the reality, but do you think it is real? No, it is not, and you know it is not. You know it is merely a story, but still you insist on crying when the scene is sad, or laugh if the scene is funny. You even take sides and choose one character over another, and you become defensive if something goes wrong in his or her part. Actually, this is merely a reflection of what is going on inside you. It points out your own dilemmas.

My purpose in talking to you about this is to make you aware so that you can witness your daily play or your daily drama. You must first be aware that all you do is merely a drama. And my recommendation is for you to witness and be aware of all that goes on around you every day. Once you have achieved this awareness, you can go to the next step of learning. So, as your guide I tell you to seek yourself which has nothing to do with your daily drama. I am simply telling you to shine your destiny, to shine your life. When I tell you not to resist, I am telling you to flow with whatever is happening around you. I am telling you to go with the flow. Maybe you will understand it by the following example.

In China there was a famous saint whose name was Hui Hy. A young poet came to him asking how he could achieve salvation, or *moksha*. The saint answered, "If you are trying to get or achieve something, never come to me." Do you see the contradiction in the saint's statement? What is the contradiction? When you ask to achieve something, you speak about the future, when in reality you are in the present. How is it possible when you are here and now to try to achieve something in the future? Know that between the future and you there is a big gap. People cannot see the contradictions in their questions. They want to achieve something, they want to get something, and they do not understand that when they say, "I want to achieve," that they are talking about the future.

When you try to achieve something, tension happens. Trying creates tension, so where there is tension there is no flow. Where there is resistance, there is no flow. The saint told him, "Never come to me if you are asking to achieve." The poet left the saint and from there he went from ashram to ashram, from guru to guru. Eventually he got so tired and so fed up with his running from place to place that he decided to come back to the same guru once again. As soon as he came, the saint asked him if he was still trying to achieve something. "No," replied the poet. I got fed up. I got tired and now I am not here to get something, I am here to be, I am here to relax."

Sometimes you put forth all of your efforts and still nothing happens. But all of a sudden when you leave effort behind you, you suddenly relax. This is what happened to Newton and to Einstein. Once they relaxed, they made many discoveries.

How did Marie Curie find out about radium? She had put forth so much effort, but still got no results. One day after trying so hard, she got fed up. She couldn't even sleep at night because she had so much tension. Trying to achieve something creates tension. There is no way to escape this. As soon as you try to achieve, it creates tension. There is no way to escape this tension. Where there is tension there is no achievement, no moksha. You cannot look at yourself because you are tense, but when you finally do look at yourself you become a totally different person and it feels as if it is not you. So one day Marie Curie dropped everything, and as soon as she let it all go, the same night she was able to sleep fully. When a person is fully, and I mean *fully,* asleep, something happens to the being, to the soul. So Marie Curie slept fully and got the formula she was searching for in her dream. Most likely, she suddenly got connected to her consciousness. She woke up, wrote down the formula, and fell asleep again. She slept and slept and slept, and when she woke up, there on her table was the formula.

So when you try to put effort into anything, you get tense. The things which cannot be achieved by effort can be achieved by relaxation. Relaxation is the key. However, people do the opposite. It seems contradictory and, in fact, it *is* contradictory. Try to go with the flow, be with yourself, and then you will see who you really are.

The universe is a play. We play different roles day after day, unaware that it is a play. You must first recognize that your present life is an ongoing drama. By knowing this you recognize that the witness is separate from this continuous drama. And although you play the role by changing into different masks to fit the situation, you know that the real you is the witness of this drama. Once you realize this, you can begin to shine your destiny, and by letting go of your trying and by living here and now in a totally relaxed state, you will achieve more than you can ever imagine.

KRIPA

Time moves on and you are wasting your breath. Still you haven't learned to love God. Your life, like a twisted dream, will one day end. Still you haven't learned to love God. As death nears, you haven't yet experienced your Self. You still haven't learned to love God. The saints tell you that in this life you are supposed to do good things. Still, you haven't learned to love God. You only know how to look at one side of life, never thinking that there is another side.

From the time we are born we begin to celebrate our birthday, but we ignore its real meaning. In India there is a proverb, and this proverb refers to the happiness we experience when our daughter and son have a birthday. We are extremely happy and rejoice on the fact that they are turning ten, fifteen, or twenty, and on and on. On one hand it is good because they are getting experience, but on the other hand this is not really an occasion for true rejoicing or happiness. Deep down, birthdays mean something else. On one hand you are happy that your son is twenty years old, but on the other hand you are not aware that the God of Death is happy too, knowing that twenty years are gone. If one's life span is sixty years, it means that twenty years are gone, and now only forty years are left. Both are happy, but lets think about it for a moment. I can't

141

understand why you are happy that your child has turned twenty. Why aren't you realizing the truth? If you realize it maybe you will begin to think about not wasting your life anymore, and you will work towards gaining something out of life. After all, life is for gaining, not for losing. You are here to gain, not to lose. This is our slogan in India.

In India I have suggested many things to the Indian people. When people come for blessings, it is an Indian tradition to say "Guruji or Maharajji, *Kripa Karo* - please bless us." Kripa means bless. But they don't understand the real meaning of Kripa. Kripa has two roots, "Kri," meaning doing, and "Pa," meaning to get. This is why I always suggest that people "do and get." "Why are you asking for my blessings?" I used to ask them. "Just do and you will get." If you will do, you will get. So this teaching is based on doing the right things. But many doings are useless. People have a hard time staying without doing anything. It is very difficult.

A little girl was playing by the bank of the river. "Rosi where are you?" her mother cried to her. "I am looking for you but I can't find you. What are you doing, Rosi?" Rosi heard her mother and she answered, "I am not doing anything." The mother replied, "No, you are doing something." "Really," Rosi cried, "I am not doing anything but lying down on the sand and enjoying myself." Rosi's mother replied, "Don't lie to me; I know you are doing something." Rosi got annoyed and started throwing rocks, and said, "I am throwing rocks, Mom." "I knew it, I knew it," said her mom. "Now stop it immediately."

So when people are enjoying nature, you cannot tolerate them. When they really enjoy life, you cannot tolerate them, but if they are doing something, you tell them to stop it immediately. This goes to show that no matter what one is doing, useful or not, you still find an excuse not to tolerate such a person.

But life has meaning only when you are involved with right doing; otherwise life has no meaning at all. If you are not on the right track, you might go on and on, but you will not achieve your goal. You might even be looking at your goal, but you still cannot reach it. Sometimes people are looking at their destination. They see it, but they cannot achieve it. That is the way society goes on. That is the way our lives go on. We see the goal; at times we even see the ultimate goal, but we cannot reach it.

If you are at the foot of Mount Everest, the highest peak in the Himalaya (and in the world), you can see it, but to climb it is very difficult. There are too many obstacles, too many difficult paths along the way. Sometimes you have to cross the edge of the mountain and if you are not aware and suddenly slip, you will fall into the abyss. Many people have tried to climb Mount Everest and have died on the way.

It is the same with you. You know your goal but you cannot reach it. Along the way there are many difficulties which need to be understood. If you want to reach your goal, you must welcome all the difficulties you encounter along the way. You might find you are lacking the courage or the confidence you need to climb, or you might find that you have no patience when you see it takes more than one day. Or perhaps you might be either too weak physically or mentally or both, and if this is the case, you might not even start your journey. These are the difficulties which must be addressed if you want to reach your goal.

Don't ask for my blessings. Instead, "do and get." I tell everyone if you do, you will get. But you have to do it the right way, by searching the right path. If you have will power, life energy, and confidence, you can cross valleys and mountains. And no matter what happens, you will get there. You might find many difficulties on your way, but you will not care. Just as the river finds its way, you too will find your way.

Learn from the river. The river comes down from the mountain without any path. It has no signpost or milestone to show it the way. But the river does have one advantage: it has current and power. And yes, it has a lot of power. Because the river is strong, it has no concern about where it will to go; it will find its own way. So if you have strong backing, you too can reach your ultimate goal. You might be weak, but if someone is behind you, you will find your own way.

Develop your courage, have confidence in yourself, and you too can make your path. Courage, strong will power and confidence will be the current you need. Be like the river and you will reach your destination. You simply need this kind of power. If you have plenty of power, you will start your journey even though in the beginning you don't see where you are going. But with confidence and will power you will move on until the goal becomes visible. When you are in the first grade, you don't know what will happen in second grade. You don't even know about first grade, but slowly you go on and on. From elementary school you move to high school, then to college, until one day you finally get your doctorate degree.

It takes confidence, patience, courage and will power to grow. In this world, nobody is powerless, and according to our teachings, the soul has infinite power. In Hindi we call the soul *atma*, and atma has infinite power. Atma is your very life. Scientists think that our body is the combination of five elements - earth, air, fire, space and water - and that the body is nothing more than the combination of these five elements. Scientists think that once the combination is gone you are dead. But I don't think so, because once the soul leaves the body, the combination is still there. So why is it that the eyes cannot see, the mouth cannot eat, the ears cannot hear and the nose cannot smell? The body is pronounced dead and cannot do anything anymore even though the combination is still there. It means that which was driving this instrument is gone. That which is gone is the soul, the atma. The atma was really the driver of this instrument.

Scientists have unsuccessfully tried to reproduce this driving force. Not only could they not reproduce the driving force, they could not reproduce the body either. They may have invented many other things. They have been successful in improving and developing some of its parts, but they have not been able to reproduce the body itself.

To increase speed, scientists invented the bicycle. But that was not enough, so they invented cars and trains. Still, they were not satisfied, so they invented airplanes, and lately, the spaceship. These new instruments are nothing more than sophisticated feet to move you to your destination more quickly.

Not only have they developed speed, they decided to develop a more powerful brain. Our brain has a lot of power. You can put billions of bits of information in it. It will stay there, but sometimes when we are tired or sleepy its stored information might not be readily accessible. This is why they invented computers. What is the computer? Nothing more than a developed brain. However, even though a computer can store billons of bits of information, it still cannot be compared to the human brain. Your brain is still more powerful because it is a unique instrument. People will go on developing more things. They have improved on your eyes by inventing binoculars, telescopes and radar. They will go on and develop more and more, but eventually they will get to the point when they cannot go any further. Soul cannot be reproduced.

Without atma you cannot see, you cannot hear, you cannot smell, you cannot taste, and you cannot touch. Nothing can happen without atma. Atma has sensation, it has feelings, and it has the power of enjoying and of suffering.

If you can understand this invisible power, you will know your Self. This power is invisible, therefore it cannot be described. Atma is like light; you think you can see the light, when in reality you cannot. However, because of light you see the things. Light itself is invisible. You cannot see the current. Can you see the current running through the electrical wires? No, you cannot. But through appropriate instruments you can detect it. So it is with the soul. The soul is more or less analogous to the electrical wires, but don't misunderstand it to be like that which you are familiar with. Soul is invisible and very powerful, and soul is you. It is said that soul has infinite power. Soul means you, and if you come to really know your *soul*, then you can have infinite power. Actually, you can do anything you want. You can change the whole nation, the whole Earth. You have that much power. Your body is the largest powerhouse because it contains *you*, the *soul*.

I used to read the *Upanishads* and in one of them I found a wonderful slogan: *Yet Pinde Tad Brahmande*. Brahmande means universe, and Pinde means body. Whatever you have in this body you will find the same thing in the cosmos, but you are not aware of your body. Your body has mountains, rivers and oceans. It is condensed like condensed juice. Many rivers are running in your body. Can you imagine that in your very little brain there are billions of bulbs? I will tell you that the brain is the most sensitive part in your body; still we do not use it. Geniuses like Newton or Einstein actually used only twenty-five percent of their brain capacity. And these are geniuses – what about us? We don't even use ten percent of our brains. Can you image if you used all of your brain? You could travel through all the universe, through all the cosmos, and you could reach Mars when satellites continue to fail. Yogis used to visit everywhere. How? They developed their brain capacities. By performing some spiritual practices, they stimulated their brains to work up to fifty percent of their capacity. You can't even imagine what could happen if the brain started working at fifty percent capacity. Even if the sun were shining, you would still see the stars. The sunlight would not be an obstacle then. As it is now, when the sun is there you cannot see the stars. The stars do not seem to be there in daylight, but by developing your brain (which is to improve your inner eye), you will be able to see the stars even in broad daylight.

I was reading once that a lady fell down from the roof and hit her head and that her brain started working in an unusual way. It is said that in broad daylight she could see not only stars, but also planets. Her sudden change became an unbearable experience and she could not find anyone to help her. She consulted many psychologists but none succeeded in helping her. If I were in her place I would have been very happy - the happiest person in the whole world! Unluckily, it happened to her and not to me.

You have to be very careful because sometimes the brain can start working very suddenly. People have even suddenly regained their eyesight. Their eyes were alright, but the connection to their brain was off, and when they accidentally hit their head, they regained their eyesight. Take a light bulb: when slightly loosened, the light goes off, but after a small adjustment it goes on again. The same principle can be applied to the brain.

Many Rishis and Munis, for the purpose of spiritual advancement, invented many spiritual practices called *sadhanas*. These practices are based on Self-discovery. However, these practices take much time and dedication. But if you want to improve, you must devote time to Self-discovery. Be patient and understand that the results for your effort might not be immediate. The right step is to start with you, by looking at yourself. Within this body there are many things to be discovered. The whole universe can be discovered within your body. If you know yourself, you will know everything and everybody. But if you don't know yourself, you will not be able to know anything.

Sometimes people want to really help others, but they cannot. Like the case of the lady who could see the stars during the day, no one could really help her. Many people want to help, but can't. They don't know themselves, and because of it they are afraid of many things. Even the greatest psychologists are afraid. I read once that Freud was afraid of ghosts. Even hearing the word ghost was enough for him to be instantly afraid. Just the mention of the word ghost would make him faint. He tried to help many people, but the only thing he could do was to help them to cope with their problems; he could not release them from their karmas. Even he could not be helped. Jung was also another great psychologist. He didn't fear ghosts, but he did fear mummies. He could never visit Egypt because of it. Just the word mummies used to scare him.

You have to find out your own weaknesses. Don't find the weaknesses of others. Being human means having weaknesses. Everybody has weaknesses. Don't think that only you or only others have weaknesses. Everybody has weaknesses, and if you look at yourself – at your own weaknesses – you will become the most intelligent person, because you will start working on them so you can fully liberate yourself from their grip.

All over the world there is only one thing wrong. Nobody is ready to look at his or her own weaknesses or mistakes. They only look at others'. If somebody only does a small wrong, they consider it to be a very big accomplishment. But if they're making any mistakes they are unwilling to see their own weaknesses. If you point a finger at others, mind that at the same time there are three fingers pointing back at you. It means that if he has one fault, then you have three times more. So your own fingers are telling the truth, but you are not willing to look at your own faults. This is why wise people tell us to look at ourselves first. If you really do it, know that you will be the most wonderful person on Earth.

Actually, in this case "person" is not the correct word to use. Person comes from the Greek word *persona*, which means mask, and mask refers to something which is not real. I prefer to use the Sanskrit word *manav*. Manav comes from Manu, the one who has given us the great Law of Humanity. Manu was the first lawgiver in the world, and the first sage to bring social reform to humans. It was Manu who wrote the book called *Manu Smriti*.

From Manu comes *manav*, and manav means the human itself. So manav comes from Manu, which means law. It is the true and complete law of existence, not only of society. Manu is the law of Self. If you can understand Manu, or the law of Self, you will be the most wonderful manav (human being) in the whole world. This is why in India we do not use the word "person"; we use "manav."

Purush is another Sanskrit word for person. "Puri shete iti purush" means "That which sleeps in the city," with city meaning "body." So purush means "that which sleeps or dwells in this body." The one who has discovered the soul is purush.

It is up to you to discover your being – your soul – which dwells in you, but is still dormant. If soul is still dormant, it means you cannot do the right thing. But if you have awakened it either by the help of someone or by your witnessing or by your watchfulness, it means you have become purush.

In discovering that which is now sleeping within us we become purush. Purush can do *purshartha* and purushartha means "right effort," and "right doing." Purushartha means "Self discovering," but Indian scholars have mistranslated purushartha by using the word "physical work." Purushartha is not physical work, but work done to discover one's Self. When you work on being aware, and when you work on being awakened, you are doing purushartha. Otherwise, your work will be merely work, labor.

For those who want to discover their being, I teach them to do purushartha. I never tell them to work. I never condemn work; after all, work is for survival. I know that for survival everybody needs to work. But this work is only physical; it has nothing to do with discovering oneself. Working for survival is not purushartha. Purushartha means you are working toward Self-discovery. So don't delay this work, because once the days and the nights are gone they are gone forever, and they will never come back.

Lord Mahavira said, "Ja ja vachai rayani, na sa padiniyatai." – "The days and the nights which have passed are forever gone. The nights and days which are past will never come back." "Dhamam hu kuna manassa safala janti raino." – "Only when doing purshartha do your days and nights have meaning, otherwise you are wasting your life." If you haven't yet experienced yourself, I recommend you to do so. Death is coming closer and closer, but still you are not aware, you are not realizing the truth. Holy persons tell you to do purushartha, to discover your real Self, and to do work for your survival. In twenty-four hours you can find one hour for Self-discovery to devote to doing purushartha. But if you can devote more than one hour, maybe several hours, you will get the real point much faster.

You need to do some spiritual practices like meditation. Meditation is the way to improve in order to reach your soul. Meditation means to merge with yourself, with your energy.

Lord Mahavira gave four words to describe meditation. Somebody visited him and asked how to reach the real point, the Godhood, and improve oneself. Lord Mahavira said, "*Thanenam*," – "Search your place." Where is your real place? Is it your house? Is it your body? Is it your mind? Is your house, your body, your mind, your eternal place? Is your brain your eternal place? The brain can be kept alive if it has oxygen, but if there is no oxygen, then after six minutes the brain will also die. So not even the brain is your eternal place. Where do you find your real place? Are your senses your real place? No, not even your senses are your real place. It is you who is speaking through your senses, who is smelling through your nose, who is seeing through your eyes. Search yourself and you will find your real place.

The questioner was very intelligent and asked, "How shall I search?" Mahavira answered again in only one word: "*Monenam*," – "Be silent." He suggested to everybody to "be silent," but his followers, his *munis*, were still speaking. The silence he was talking about is different. It is not the silence of speech. Speaking has no such meaning to the word "silence." Maybe you have taken the vow of silence, but in your mind the marketplace is still going on. That is not silence. Lord Mahavira meant to be silent from anger, from pride, from jealousy, ego, and all the lower qualities. Silence yourself, and don't let your thoughts go on changing like TV channels. Be silent from your thoughts. That is what silence means.

But the questioner was so intelligent and asked again, "How can I be silent?" Mahavira spoke one more word: "*Jhanenam*," – "Meditate." By meditating you can be silent, but you have to learn meditation. The questioner said, "Please don't tell me any more stories. First you said, 'thanenam,' then you sad 'monenam.' I don't want to listen any more. Please answer the last question for me."

"I asked how to search, and you said to be silent. I asked how to be silent, and you suggested again to meditate. But as to how to meditate, I don't understand anything you said." Mahavira answered, "*Apanam bosirami*,"–"Dissolve yourself, forget yourself."

You can do everything, but you cannot forget yourself. That is why Rosi started throwing stones. To forget oneself means to act like a dead person, and to act like a dead person is the hardest thing to do. You cannot surrender; you cannot act like a dead person because a dead person never acts. You are sitting silently and somebody comes and starts calling you bad names and suddenly you begin to boil inside. You cannot stand it, so you react. It means you cannot forget yourself – you are affected. When you cannot forget yourself, you cannot meditate; when you don't meditate, you cannot be silent; when you are not silent, you cannot search your real place.

Mahavira gave four suggestions so you can search your real place. You must be silent. To be silent you must meditate. To meditate you must forget yourself, at least for a while. If you do it for a longer time it will be difficult to live in society, but you can at least begin by doing it for a while.

You can forget yourself on the weekend, but your weekends are just as busy. Weekends are wonderful, but you become even more active when you actually need to rest. That is why the government suggested that you have two days off.

If you can practically forget yourself and be silent one day you will discover your real place. Flow and learn from the river. Flow without making any ripples, any sounds, no thoughts, and no TV channels. Then you can learn to meditate. If you can do it you learn so many things.

Time moves on and you are wasting your breaths. Still you haven't learned to love God. Your life is like a twisted dream, and one day it will end. Still you haven't learned to love God. As death nears you, you haven't yet experienced your Self. Still you haven't learned to love God. In this life, the saints tell you that you are supposed to do good things. Still you haven't learned to love God. You only know how to look at one side of life, never thinking there is another side.

You have to start looking at the other side of existence. If you rejoice in celebrating your birthdays, or if you find ways to feel content and happy, remember: if you do not learn to love God, all of your rejoicing will only give you limited experience. Life is more than this. Celebrate your children's birthdays, but remember that the God of Death is celebrating too. Realize the other side, and your life will be complete.

BOW AND LOOK AT YOUR HEART

God is inside each and every one of us. God is not separate from us. We only have to learn where to look. If we humbly lower our eyes towards our hearts, there we will see God. When you want to see your beloved, bow your head towards your heart. When you want to see God, do the same. God's creation is like a dance and God is like a dancer. The dance can never be separated from the dancer. Creation cannot be separate from God and if God is divine, creation is also divine. Awaken this truth, and once the dancer and dance are one, you and God will be also one.

Awakening to one's greatest possibility is the ultimate goal of your birth. However, for some people it might be easier to awaken than it is for others. Actually, you will find that in this world there are four types of people. The first kind of person merely needs to be called by his or her name to be awakened. The second needs only a sprinkling of water. The third one needs a real shaking, while the forth one needs to have the whole bucket of water poured on him. But there is one condition: once awake, you need to be even more attentive and aware of each one of your actions. Criticizing others for not being at your same level is very detrimental. And if this is the case it is actually best if you remain asleep and ignorant.

The example of the Muslim fakir who went on a pilgrimage with his son is a good one. The fakir, who was actually a saint, took his son to Mecca and Medina. They had walked a long distance and rested at night along the way. At sunrise, while the other pilgrims remained fast asleep, the father and the son performed their morning prayer. His son was really bothered by the laziness of the other pilgrims and started complaining to his father about them, and about the fact that they were more willing to spend their time sleeping rather than praying before continuing their journey to the holy place. After hearing much complaint from his son, the father turned to him and said, "I wish you would be asleep too as they are, this way I would not have to put up with your complaining, and your mind would not be filled with these evil thoughts."

To be awakened and to realize the God within is wonderful, but to be critical of others who are not yet awakened negates even your own awakening. Being critical is a negative quality, and we need to be mindful of it.

God is not only within us, but also within each and every living being. However, to see it and realize it we must be humble. By increasing all the qualities of love, non-violence and compassion, you will know that all creation is divine. Don't repress or control any of your negative emotions or thoughts: otherwise you will poison yourself. Simply increase all the positive qualities of love, non-violence, compassion, etc.

The example of how to shorten a line drawn on a blackboard might bring clarity to you. Once I asked some children if they could shorten the line drawn on the blackboard without touching it. No one knew what I meant and could not figure it out. After few moments, I picked up a piece of chalk and drew a longer line above it, and the children understood. This is also how you should handle your negative thoughts and emotions. You have to increase your love, your compassion and be non-violent. You should not return violence with violence, hate with hate, anger with anger. Rather, you should increase your *love*, and your lower qualities will automatically decrease.

There is a beautiful saying: "If you can build a house by laying bricks over bricks, if you can compose the most wonderful symphony by combinations of the seven main notes, know that by increasing your love towards all living beings you will realize Supreme Love." Be more humble and look down at your heart. There you will see God.

REALIZATION BRINGS HAPPINESS

John D. Rockefeller was one of the richest men on Earth; he had so much money that it couldn't even be counted. He was so rich he was probably making a million dollars per minute. One day he became very sick and he felt he might die soon. So, before dying he decided to go out boating on the ocean and really enjoy the day. He did, but while sitting on his seat the boat unexpectedly capsized. A big roaring wave engulfed the boat, making it sink. Rockefeller found himself in a very difficult situation and thought, "The boat is sinking, and because I am in it I am sinking along with it. The boat has nothing to do with death, but I feel that because of it my death is near." Suddenly, the idea of earning and losing money disappeared from his mind. The moment was very crucial, and his whole life was in jeopardy. He was left with no other choice but to go deep within his thoughts. He began to think, "What is the meaning of earning millions or billions of dollars, or for that matter, to lose millions or billions of dollars? Nothing makes sense anymore – none of this has any meaning." He went so deep into his thoughts that instead of panicking he began to relax fully, and suddenly help came and he was saved.

His positive attitude brought him into his depths and he became *swasth*, meaning a person who is fully in himself or in herself and who begins to realize himself or herself. He realized a powerful truth. Seeing his death nearing, his whole outlook changed. Whenever this happens to a person, realization is certain. Such moments are very precious because they can bring one to question life's real meaning. Do you think there is meaning in being the richest or the poorest person on Earth? In those moments when you see life coming to an end, such preoccupations disappear. Reality has nothing to do with how rich or how poor you are. Rockefeller's realization brought him a lot of happiness. He became relaxed and was able to flow with what was happening and because of it he was saved. Realization always breeds happiness. There is no way that it cannot. After any realization, a person becomes happy, but if you do not realize anything, this happiness cannot be experienced.

Even a common person, after having worked very hard for the whole week, becomes very happy to know that the weekend has come and he or she can spend the whole time resting and enjoying their life. He or she might spend hours and hours alone in his or her room feeling totally relaxed. On the other hand, a person who lives in luxury might, if by misunderstanding, be held prisoner in his or her own home, and he or she might experience terror instead. Even though he or she is surrounded by luxuries and comforts, under those conditions it feels like being in hell. When freedom is taken, no matter what one has around oneself, all of those things lose all value, especially if your life is being threatened.

Because Rockefeller began to think in those terms, he became swasth. His realization was deep and he came to understand the real value of life, and because of it I am sure he died very happy. Anyone who has this kind of realization becomes free. But if there is no realization there will be no relaxation, even if the person is surrounded by luxuries and all kinds of facilities. Things cannot make a person relaxed or happy: only realization can.

FLOW WITH THE FLOW

There was a popular saint in India whose name was Baba Mehar. He was clairvoyant. One day, he was scheduled to take a trip and he refused to board the plane. Both airport authorities and his disciples wondered why all of a sudden he had changed his mind. Baba Mehar could not give any explanation. He only knew he couldn't go. The plane took off, and it crashed soon after. Another similar incident happened once when he was to board a train. Once again he refused. Baba Mehar knew ahead of time what was going to happen. Because of this ability to know the future, Baba Mehar became quite popular among the people. But were his decisions right? Consider that Jesus did not interfere with his destiny.

When Jesus was to be crucified, he uttered, "God, what are you doing? Why are you forsaking me? What are you allowing them to do?" He was very angry, and his ego overshadowed his judgment. Overpowered by his ego, he felt he was greater than God, but he soon realized his mistake and said, "God, forgive me and forgive them for not knowing what they are doing." Jesus surrendered and allowed himself to move with the flow. No longer interfering with the outcome, that's when he became The Christ.

To be a Christ is not easy. It is very difficult. I am not in agreement with

Baba Mehar's decision. He could have allowed himself to flow in the hands of God, in the hands of Nature. If we accept life, why can't we accept death? It means he still had ego. Jesus still had ego too, but as soon as his ego dissolved he became The Christ. It is very hard to move with the flow. We have a difficult time letting go of ourselves, so we resist. By resisting, the ego gets the upper hand. This is why we have a hard time leaving ourselves in the hands of nature or God.

One day, a grandfather was praying. After finishing his prayers he came to his grandchildren. The children were young, ranging in age from three to five years. He said to them, "God can fulfill everything I ask for. Whatever I need, God fulfills it for me." One grandchild came to him and said, "Grandpa can you ask God for a little toy for me?" And do you know what the grandfather's answer was? "Why do you ask for a toy? A toy is just a toy!" But for the child, a toy is everything. Maybe for grown-ups it is merely a toy, but for a child a toy is the most precious thing. Prayer can happen when we flow with the flow in the hands of God.

Swami Vivekananda was Ramakrishna Paramahansa's (*Paramahansa* means Great Soul) only disciple, and the first yogi to travel abroad to the United States. He was sent as the Indian representative to the World Religion Conference in Chicago. Vivekananda was not familiar with any Western countries or any Western traditions. This was his first experience in the West. Chicago at that time of the year was very cold – icy cold – and Vivekananda had no idea where to go. Somehow he managed to get a taxi, but he still got lost. He asked for help, and an old lady gave him shelter for the night. The next day he came to the conference. When it was his turn to speak he had only five minutes to deliver his speech. There were many delegates from many countries, so the speakers had limited time to present their views. His speech, which was about Indian mythology and religion, was most powerful. It was very enthusiastically received. People became so intrigued with him that they begged him to go on. This was the first time that Indian religions were introduced in the United States. People were mesmerized by his speech, and his five-minute presentation ended up being one hour and thirty minutes. People loved him.

Swami Vivekananda's father died when he was a child, leaving the family in great debt. People were constantly pressuring him and his family to pay back the money his father had borrowed. His mother had very little money, and Vivekananda was still a student earning no money. Whatever he earned was barely enough to feed the two of them. Many nights he had to go to sleep without any food because there was only enough food to feed one person. He did not want his mother to know, so he would tell her that his friend, who was a very good cook, had prepared the best meal for him, when in fact he had had nothing to eat and had to sleep with an empty stomach several nights in a row. One day, someone advised him to go see Ramakrishna Paramahansa. Paramahansa was very close to Divine Mother, and it was known that Divine Mother always fulfills all wishes. Vivekananda took the advice to see Paramahansa. He came to him and asked for his help. Paramahansa simply said, "Pray, and when you are in prayer ask the Divine Mother to fulfill your wish." Vivekananda followed the advice and he went very deep into prayer. Every time he was in prayer, the Divine Mother would stand in front of him and ask him if he needed anything. But every time he was deep in prayer he felt so complete that he could never ask for anything. When he came back to the teacher, the teacher would want to know if he had asked the Divine Mother to fulfill his wish. "No, I couldn't do it," he would reply. "Why?" Paramahansa asked. "Whenever I am deep in prayer I feel I am the richest person in the whole world. It is only when I come back that I find I am still poor." His teacher suggested for him to try again the next day. So he did. But every time he was in that state, he could not ask at all.

Actually, prayer happens only when your whole being is involved in the action. If your whole being is involved in any action, it becomes prayer. Your whole being has to be involved, not just the mind, not just the body. I am saying the *whole being*. It is a flowing. It is like floating on water and you allow your body to be fully transported. You do nothing but let yourself be transported. You just surrender to the water while you allow the water to carry you. You don't resist, because if you do you might drown.

Asking is not prayer. Really, once you are fully in prayer you can never ask God for anything. Asking is begging for something. You beg for money, for fame, for your children's happiness, for a girlfriend or boyfriend. Or maybe you ask God for a good husband or a good wife, and so on and so on. So many things are there to be asked for, but remember: all of your asking has nothing to do with prayer. Swami Vivekananda, as soon as he dissolved into prayer, became the king of kings. You too can become the king of kings.

Even Jesus, the King of Kings, was very poor. When he was to be crucified there was no food in him. For the Last Supper there was only one piece of bread, which had to be divided among twelve disciples. Just one piece of bread, and still he was the King of Kings. But at the time of his crucifixion he forgot his place, and he resisted the condition. In resisting, he was simply Jesus. But as soon as he realized what he was doing he asked his father's forgiveness, not only for himself, but also for those who were killing him. His whole being was involved in the action and that's when prayer happened and he became *The Christ*. That is why Christians firmly believe that on the third day Christ was resurrected from the dead.

When action is full, action is then with God. And in merging with God, you never die. But let me tell you, this happening, this transformation, can never be intellectually understood. It can only be realized. Words cannot describe the depth of this transformation. No language is adequate enough to convey what this means because language is incomplete. Language is a linear expression, and any linear expression is the most incomplete thing in the whole world. The reality is that in human life all the possibilities are there.

In the newborn child all the possibilities are present. So if all possibilities are present, it means the child can be, or can turn out to be, anything. In the same moment he can be on one hand a monk or a great leader, or on the other hand he can be a drug addict, a killer, or the most violent person. The possibilities to be a Hitler or Saddam Hussein, someone who can kill lots of people, or a god, are present all at once. In the newborn all these possibilities are there. Life is like all the possibilities already present in the newborn. All these possibilities are what prayer is. Prayer is not linear like language is: it is life itself. With language, you can convey one possibility at a time, while in the newborn all the possibilities are there at once. When you dissolve or lose yourself in the hand of nature, all possibilities can happen in the same moment.

Have you ever noticed a baby falling? The baby does not get injured like an adult would. The baby's bones remain intact, while in adults the bones will easily fracture. Why? Because grown people resist when they fall. Where there is resistance there is ego, and ego breaks. But with the child the possibility of a fracture is much less, unless there is something in the way to cause it. Where there is resistance there is no Christ. Where there is resistance, there is no Krishna.

Lord Krishna, too, surrendered and accepted his death. He knew already that the next time he was to cross the jungle someone was going to shoot an arrow through his foot. Yet, he entered the jungle. He did not resist and still went in. In the night, while Krishna was resting, someone shot the arrow into his foot, and Krishna left his body. Even though Krishna knew the outcome of entering the jungle, he still chose not to resist nature. Why interfere with nature? It is best to flow with it. If you can really learn how to flow, you will never be in misery, and you will never feel pain and suffering ever again.

Let me give you an example. Swami Ramakrishna Paramahansa had cancer, and you know how painful it is to die of cancer. His devotees constantly encouraged him to ask the Divine Mother, with whom he was very close, to heal the cancer. He used to say, "The problem is, when I am with Ma or with Goddesses there is no pain – no cancer. It is only when I come back that the cancer is there. How can I bring myself to ask for the cancer to be healed when the pain disappears every time I am in prayer? I do not understand what you want me to ask for."

When a person dissolves himself or herself, he or she feels no pain, no suffering, and no misery ever again. And when deep in prayer he or she becomes a Christ, a Krishna, a Buddha or God. Maybe at the beginning there will still be some ego. However, as soon you realize this is not the way, you will begin to dissolve it from the deepest part of yourself, your consciousness. Then everything becomes a miracle. A child can get a toy. Grownups can have anything they want. But everything has to come from the deepest core of their being, and it has to be felt wholeheartedly. If you do anything wholeheartedly, it becomes prayer. That action is no longer an action. It is prayer. It is divine. It is something indescribable.

WALKING ALONE

Once I read a book by a famous writer in which he talks about our traveling. In his book he states that in the course of our lives we travel with so many different people. He stresses the fact that we never take the time to be comfortable enough to travel with ourselves.

He goes on to say that we travel with our friends, we travel with our families, and with our relatives. He further mentions all sorts of people we travel and do business with. We do business with strangers, we do business with friends, we do business with relatives, and yes, we do business with a partner too. In other words, our attention is constantly diverted from ourselves to others, implying that in the end all will be left behind. Nobody and nothing goes with us; we are born alone and we die alone.

Sartre said, "Hell is other people." But what do you do instead? You constantly cling to others, mainly because of your lack of self-confidence and courage. You need to improve yourselves and know that you are special. Merely understanding this very truth will make you grow. And in facing the fact that you are born alone and that you will die alone you will lose the fear associated with being alone and you will become the most

171

beautiful person on Earth. Because of your lack of courage you immerse yourselves in doing things with friends, relatives, etc. as an escape. You don't even want to be reminded that when the journey ends you will not be carrying anyone along with you. Real confidence and trust are gained when you experience your inner and outer aloneness. Know that when aloneness, stillness and peace are achieved the possibility for moksha, the liberated state of being is also attained.

I remember something I read about which happened twenty-five hundred years ago. A great king, who had conquered many lands, heard that moksha was the one last thing to be conquered. The King knew of a great Master, Lord Mahavira, and was told to visit him and inquire how to achieve moksha. When Lord Mahavira, who was an enlightened master, heard the king's request, he must have been laughing inside knowing very well that moksha could not be conquered, nor bought. However, Lord Mahavira did not deny the king's desire. Instead, he directed him to another person. The king became very happy and thought it would be easier to buy the person rather than moksha itself. Instead of going to the man himself, the king first sent his messenger to him. The man told the messenger that if the king wanted to see him that he had to come to him personally. So the king came to the man's door and asked him personally if he could buy moksha from him. The man politely answered, "You can buy me, but you cannot buy moksha." Moksha cannot be bought; moksha can only happen. Moksha means that state in which you are fully liberated from everything and are in ecstasy and bliss all the time. "No," replied the King, "Lord Mahavira, who is an enlightened master, told me I could buy it from you. How much do you want me to pay you for it?" he asked the man. The king said, "What if I give you a million dollars?" (Or whatever the currency was at that time.) "One Million?" the man answered. Then the king replied, "What about ten million, or what if I give you the whole kingdom!" The man had achieved moksha but had no riches; he was a poor man and could barely manage for food. He was surviving hand to mouth, and the king was ready to give him his whole kingdom just for moksha, and he refused it. In Buddhism, moksha is called nirvana. Nirvana or moksha or liberation are one in the same. "Even if you give me the whole universe, you cannot purchase moksha or nirvana or liberation," said the man. "But let me tell you what you need to do. You have to sit here with me, close your eyes and disconnect yourself from everything and everyone. Maybe then the possibility for moksha will happen." The king said, "This is my problem; I cannot sit, I have to run, I have to walk, I have to do things all the time, and I cannot stay still." "But moksha can only happen in stillness, when you are mentally and physically still," replied the man.

Meditation can neither be done nor bought. Meditation is not something you do; it can happen only by your realization, by your stillness, by your peace and calmness. When everything inside becomes still and calm, then something might happen. When you are in this state completely, the whole universe begins to help.

The night Buddha decided to become an ascetic, his whole being was fully still and silent. No one knew of his plan, not even his charioteer. In fact, in the middle of the night, Buddha woke up his charioteer, trusting that he wouldn't tell anyone of his plan. The horse he chose was the fastest and strongest horse. In the scriptures it is said that when this horse walked, the sound of his steps could be heard twelve miles away, meaning that everyone could have been awakened by it. In addition to this inconvenience, the gate to the city had to also be opened. In those days, walls with only one exit surrounded cities. But that night the gate was easily opened without awakening anyone and everything turned out in Buddha's favor. His escape was effortlessly executed without trouble and without awakening anyone, all because Buddha was fully in that state of stillness and calmness. Yes, the universe showered gifts on him, aiding him in fleeing the palace unnoticed.

The whole universe helps if you can help yourself. But people try to help everything and everybody else except themselves. The real thing is to help oneself. The saying, "God helps those who help themselves" is the right thing to do, so always remember it. A guru points the finger to the moon but you have to open your eyes to see the moon. If you do not open your eyes, it does not mean anything. God cannot be seen then. What happens is that people cling to the guru's finger, or to his/her words, or to the scriptures. The teacher is here only to guide you so you can gain the confidence, courage, and the strength you need to walk and see the moon all on your own. When you do, you will blossom like a flower and you will become the most wonderful person. It is true that all of our collections remain here; nothing and no one can be taken with us. The possibility for moksha to happen is right here and now.

I remember once when I was in Idyllwild, at a children's camp. I was teaching them that if you have eyes to see and if your eyes are open you can see God here, right now. Otherwise it is impossible. One student stood up and said, "I do not believe it. God is nowhere." "I agree with you," I told him, and I made him come forward and write those words: "God is nowhere" on the blackboard. I made him read the words out loud so that the other children could hear them too. God is nowhere. I approached the blackboard and simply put a little comma after the "w" and asked the student to read it again. To his surprise, the same words he wrote now had a completely different meaning. The little comma changed the whole significance and the "nowhere" had become "now here." God is now here. This is the problem; if you could only stop, it could happen here and now. Physically, mentally or by thoughts, God could be right now here. It is like the water in a pond or in a lake, it has no ripple, and no high tide like the ocean has. It is completely still; it is not even flowing. It is with this stillness that God is now here. Here and now can happen very easily, because you are not separated from it.

If you came to me to buy moksha, I would also tell you that it cannot be bought, but it can happen. When moksha happens, bliss will be endless. It is not like happiness that comes and goes. Once bliss happens, it stays with you forever and it is indescribable. I cannot describe it to you. Moksha is the most beautiful thing that could happen in your life, but you have to realize it, you have to experience it. You cannot come to me and ask me to make it happen for you. I can only point my finger to the moon and make you realize you must not cling to my finger, but see the moon. To know what an apple tastes like, you must have a taste of it. But you are so smart that without having tasted the apple even once you might even write theories, maybe even a big thesis, on how an apple tastes. You will give your best explanation, saying that it may be like sugar, maybe like a candy or whatever you have known that is sweet. But a theory or a thesis is not the reality. To really explain what an apple tastes like, you must have had the experience. This is why researchers and scientists can write books about the apple, but reality or truth cannot be described. It cannot be told. As soon as you tell the truth, truth is already a lie. Lao-Tzu said truth cannot be told. It can be tasted, it can be experienced, but it cannot be told. You might understand this one example. If I ask you what time it is, you might say it is ten minutes to twelve. But as soon you say that it is ten minutes to twelve, you are already lying because the time has changed by the time you say it. Truth cannot be told; not even time can be told. Truth is subtler than this, and moksha is even subtler.

So the more you listen to these examples, the more you can experience calmness, peace, and serenity, the closer you will come. Maybe one day moksha will happen to you. I am always praying for reality to happen to the people who sit with me.

A THREE-STORY HOUSE

Your body is your house, your abode, and it is beautiful. This house is made of three stories. The first story goes from the feet to the waist. The second story goes from the waist to the throat. The third story is from the throat to the top of the head.

The first story is the basement where you store things. Any waste material is being recycled and eliminated there.

The second story, which is from your waist to your throat, has a very different function. Its function is digestion. Here everything gets digested to maintain the house in proper order and in proper condition. Both the first and the second stories are of great importance. But the third story, which goes from throat to head, is even more beautiful.

The purpose of the third story is to take care of everything that goes on in your body, mind and brain. It is the body's headquarters with its conglomeration of offices. Here you attend to all business and phone calls. Your two ears are your telephones. Your two eyes are your telescopes. These two telescopes are very influential too. They help you see very far. In fact they are so powerful that you can see millions of miles away. Do you know how far away stars are? Not even the moon is that far. And these two telescopes take you all the way to the stars. Can you imagine what could happen if your consciousness were open fully and every single pore began to see? You might go crazy seeing the whole universe. This is what is called *Brahmananda* or *Keval Jnan*.

What is Keval Jnan? Keval Jnan is "enlightenment," and when enlightenment happens, not only can your two telescopes see, but also every pore of your body sees. This means that each single cell has awakened. Scientifically, it has been proven that every cell in your body has its own brain. In fact, your body is nothing more than the combination of cells, which by multiplying have formed the body. There are seven million cells in the body, maybe even more. Imagine if all those cells, which have independent brains, began to work all at once. What would happen? Do you think you could handle it?

Someone asked Asanga, Buddha's disciple, who had already achieved enlightenment, why he was constantly laughing. Asanga didn't answer. Instead he laughed even more. People laughed with him. Then someone else asked if he could explain what enlightenment was like. But Asanga kept on laughing. Someone else, disturbed by this behavior, seriously asked him, "Why do you keep on laughing? We don't see Buddha laughing so much. Why do you laugh so much?" Finally, Asanga explained, "I'm laughing because of my ignorance. I'm laughing because I realized I didn't achieve anything new – it was always with me. This knowledge, this enlightenment was always with me. It was always in the palms of my hands and I did not know I was holding such a precious thing with me at all times. I was lacking the vision to see, and all because of my ignorance. Everything was with me, but my ignorance did not allow me to

see. I was not able to recognize it. This is why I am laughing so much."
Enlightenment is merely the recognition of what you already are.

When you recognize that you hold the truth and that everything is within
your reach, you will also realize that this power is within your reach too. It
has always been with you and it will always be with you. The ball is in
your court: it is you who has the power to roll it. It is not God who comes
and does it for you. No, it is you. You can reveal the truth.

Asanga, the enlightened seer, was right. I am also telling you that if your
two little eyes can see so far, imagine if your whole being – your whole
consciousness – were open fully. Just imagine what you could see! Could
you tolerate it? If you could see everything clearly, could you take it? This
is why enlightenment is very difficult to take. As soon as you see the
whole world, the intensity will be overwhelming. Both the good and the
bad will jump out at you. The majority of people in this world are bad and
all of their evil actions will become visible to the enlightened person. To
achieve enlightenment is not easy. The capacity is in you. Just recognize
the power of these two telescopes or eyes. They have a lot of power, but
this power must be realized. Your nose and mouth also have their own
powerful functions.

Your body is a beautiful instrument. In it all possibilities are hidden, but
the truth is that it is not eternal and it is not yours: it is merely rented. If
this is not realized, you will remain in ignorance, in darkness. One day,
when the time comes, you will have to leave it behind. Permanent things
cannot decay, cannot be destroyed, or be taken away from you.
Intellectually, you know this already. Anything you rent one day needs to
be vacated. You have seen it happening in the material world time and

time again. However, even though your body can decay, it is also the doorway to realizing spiritual truth. You know whoever takes birth one day has to die. No one is spared from death, because the body is not eternal; in this body there is no permanency. It is a mysterious and unexplainable experience. It is the paradox in which truth can be realized.

Your body is not eternal, but soul is. Light is eternal, but body is not. It might be here today, and tomorrow it is gone. We are all waiting in a big line. Somebody's number might come today, another might come tomorrow, or maybe after one hundred years. One hundred years or one day makes no difference. Basically they are the same. It is just a span of time...it makes no difference. It can only make a difference if someone tries to open his or her consciousness. When someone works on opening his or her consciousness, only then death has no meaning. In India, a saint's death is always celebrated, and it does not matter if the saint is young or old. People know how much effort was put forth for the advancement of the soul, and this is why their death is celebrated.

Intellectually, you know that this body is rented, but that is not enough. You must know it and realize it at a deeper level. But for you to realize this truth is not important. This is the reason why as soon as you got this body you became so egoistic, so proud and so violent, and all of your lower qualities started to surface. Why did you choose to become so egoistic about something which is merely rented? I could understand if this three-story house were yours forever, but for something you merely rent, how could you be so egoistic? Be wise and think about this for a moment. If this body were not yours, how could "your" children, father and mother be yours? Yes, it is a loaded question, but you must find the answer. It is all right to live with people, parents and children, and give affection and love. It is fine to do that. Also to fulfill your responsibilities and duties is also fine. But deep down you must accept that no one belongs to you and that you will either have to leave them or they will leave you.

Consider an old lady, who, after years of trying to bear a child, somehow around the age of fifty gave birth to a baby boy. After five years, the child died, but she could not accept his death and cried day and night. Frantically she went from place to place, holding the child in her arms in hope of finding someone who could bring him back to life. She visited all kinds of doctors without any success. People who knew her felt sad for her. She couldn't give up.

One day someone told her that maybe Buddha, the Enlightened One, could help to bring her child back to life. She took the suggestion and she brought the little body to Buddha and she explained her situation and said, "I am coming from so far and my hope is that you can bring my son back to life. You are enlightened and I was told if anyone could bring my only son back to life you could." "Yes, I can help, but you first have to fulfill a condition," Buddha replied. "I will do anything you ask of me," the lady said. "No matter what it is, if you ask me to bring the stars to you, I will go to any extent in order to have my only child with me alive." "You do not need to go that far," Buddha said. "My request is simple. Go to town and go to every single house, knock at their doors and ask simply for a little food and bring it to me, but with one condition that it can only be from that house in which death has never occurred. Only this much I am asking of you. Bring me just a little food from that house in which no person has died and I assure you I will bring your son back to life." "Sure," she said, and she left Buddha, went to the town and began to knock at everyone's door asking for some food. Everyone was willing to help her, but no one could fulfill her wish.

After enquiring if anyone had ever died in their household she found that no household had been spared death. Inevitably, the answer was: "Yes, my father died, my mother died." In the next household, someone would say, "My child died," and on and on. She went crazy. She went to every single door but she couldn't find a single family in which no one had died. She came back to Buddha and even Buddha couldn't help. In his compassion he told her that not even an enlightened person could bring her son or anyone else back to life once death had occurred.

When a person is dead, he is dead and you must accept it. We have to accept this truth, so what is the sense of being egoistic? When death knocks at your door, you have to empty the house. It is best you start praying and become a seeker instead. Don't wait until it is too late. Understand and realize this truth. But if you are not a true seeker, you will never understand it. Let me tell you a little truth, but first let me ask you a question: Why do people pray to God? They pray because they believe that God is almighty and all-powerful and will take care of everything. They firmly believe in God, but I will tell you that God will never help you unless you start helping yourself. I will assure you that God only helps those who help themselves. If your intention is never to help yourself, God will never help you either. You have to help yourself. This is why the first thing that Indian mythology teaches is *purushartha*, meaning "effort." If you don't put forth effort, know that nothing else will help either, and if even if by chance help comes your way, it will slip from you. It is better to put forth effort. Actually, God has sent many to help you, but you did not recognize the people.

This reminds me of a story. There was a flood and a man was hanging from the branch of a little tree. Trying to save himself from the current, the man was praying, "God, save me, you are the savior, the Almighty; I believe in you, please, please help me, help me." Suddenly, a boat came by. It was full of people, but fortunately there was still space available for one more person. The boat slowed down and came to the man's rescue. People invited the man into the boat, but the man refused and said, "I believe God is my savior. I will be fine because God will save me." So they left. The man continued with his prayer of "God will save me." A helicopter searching to rescue anyone came by. They saw him hanging from the tree. The current was very strong and the tree could fall at any moment. The helicopter stopped there and the people on the helicopter offered to bring him aboard. Again he refused because he firmly believed that God himself would come to save him. "I have full faith in God, and God will never let me die," he said. They also gave up and left. Finally, another fellow on a big log came by. He also offered to save the man. Such a little tree could fall at any time. "Come with me," he insisted, "and you will be saved." "No," the man replied, "I believe in God, and God will save me." He also gave up and left. Finally, the tree couldn't take it any longer and washed away in the flood and the man died. Somehow, his prayers took him to God. As soon as he saw God, he started yelling at him. "I believed in you, so why didn't you save me? I heard that you were the savior and you let me die instead. I kept on praying up to the last moment." Do you know what God's reply was? "I sent you three people and gave you three chances, but you did not hear anything. I sent you a boat, I sent you a helicopter, and I sent you a big log, but you did not put forth any effort. How could I save you?" This is the truth – God helps those who help themselves.

God sends many opportunities and many people our way, but it has to be us who acknowledges them. You have to understand that if you do not put forth any effort or do any purushartha, you are not going to be saved. Christians say that Jesus is your savior, but no matter what they say, Jesus cannot save you unless you put forth the effort to save yourself. Yes, God sends you all these people, but it has to be you who recognizes God's signals. Divine intervention is there all the time, but are you wise enough to take advantage of it? This is what effort or purushartha means: it means to keep your vision clear to recognize when God's help comes your way. What does the word "save" mean? It means that you have to search your real Self, and know who you really are. Only then will you be saved.

In Greek mythology, there was a goddess that people came to worship all the time. One day, many people gathered around the goddess to pray when suddenly a big sound from the *akash* came, saying, "Socrates is the most knowledgeable person in the world. Go to him and ask for his guidance." People listened and together went to Socrates' house. They knocked at his door, and when he opened it he said, "Such a big crowd, why did you come here?" "The goddess declared that you are the wisest person on Earth," they said, "and we came to get your guidance!" "You might be mistaken," Socrates said. "Maybe the goddess meant someone else." They left Socrates and the next day they all came again to see the goddess. The same thing happened: the goddess again told them to visit Socrates, the person they had visited the day before, being that he was the wisest man alive. So they left and came to Socrates' house again. Once more, Socrates said, "Why are you coming to see me again? I told you I am not the one. But I am sure of one thing: I am sure of my ignorance. I do not know anything else but my ignorance. I only know that much. I know my ignorance and nothing else." They said, "Oh, if he is ignorant, how can he

184

guide us?" So they went back to the *devi*, the goddess, and the goddess declared again that Socrates was the wisest person in the world.

The person who can recognize his or her ignorance is the wisest person in the whole world. The person who is considered the most knowledgeable is actually the most ignorant person on the face of the Earth. The people finally understood why Socrates told them those things. This is the truth. The person who does not recognize his or her inner ignorance will not be able to realize truth either. Ignorance is the biggest block. It prevents us from seeing through anything. It is like a big wall which stops us from seeing the truth.

Albert Einstein was walking on the beach once. Someone recognized him and knew how wise he was. Einstein was a little man, but his head was very big. The person approached him. He was so pleased to have the opportunity to meet him in person and said, "For years I have been eager to meet you and I felt that the day I met you it would be my luckiest day, and look, today you are with me." Albert Einstein responded, "My friend, maybe you recognize me and you think that I am so wise, but let me tell you one thing – knowledge is like an ocean, and my knowledge is just like a grain of sand. This is how much I know."

Can you believe Albert Einstein could make such a statement? I think that all knowledgeable people do not consider they know everything. Can you imagine if your consciousness were open fully, and you blossomed and every single pore of your body could see the whole universe? What would that be like? It can happen, but you must begin now by putting forth effort and doing purushartha.

Your first step is to realize that your body is rented and that one day it will have to go. Learn all you can about this three-story house and recognize that this beautiful rental property has great possibilities hidden in it. Realize that one day when death comes and knocks at your door, you must vacate this house. Recognize everything and try to be a true seeker, and if you really become a seeker, true knowledge and enlightenment will not be far from you. It is just like being inside a room and enlightenment is waiting outside the door. A true seeker becomes silent, not from words, but from anger, from violence, from emotions, pain, suffering, ignorance and from all the lower qualities. This makes you a true seeker, and a true seeker one day will be able to open his or her consciousness fully. Know that enlightenment and wisdom is the absence of all lower qualities and that in their absence truth is realized.

TO BE SPIRITUAL

The word spiritual comes from spirit, and by spirit I don't mean that you have spirit or inspiration. By spirit I mean soul; therefore, to know your soul, to know your Self, is to be spiritual. But to follow the spiritual path is very difficult. To know anything else is much easier than to know oneself. To have expertise on any subject, you don't need much. You only need some books to do your research. Any information you need is readily available. You have history books, you have science books; name it and you can find it. You have books on all sorts of subjects. But to know *you*, there are no books available. You might find a guide to guide you to the path, but the path is walked alone. The path is unknown and it has to be made by you. The teacher can only guide you to its entrance where you enter alone and where you flow on your own.

You might argue with me and totally disagree with this statement by saying you already know yourself. But that is not true. What you know of yourself is your body, your occupation, and the friends around you. You know what is going on in the world from watching TV and reading the daily news. But all this is not you. This is all about others. Yes, even your body is considered *other*. In knowing others, there is no secret. But if you know your Self, I am telling you, you can know everything else. You will know all the secrets of the universe.

So grow spiritually. And if you want to have a purpose, make spiritual growth your purpose. Religion has done a lot of good for humanity, but a lot of damage has come out of it too. To realize yourself you don't need religion, you need to find your spiritual path and flow in it fully.

In the next century you will see there will be more and more people growing spiritually. I feel very happy about this. Things are changing. Only ten or twelve years ago, less than one percent of the Earth's population was growing spiritually. But today it has increased already ten percent. Can you imagine in this new century what can happen? Even if only twenty percent of the people alive today can grow spiritually, the whole world's ideas will be changed. There will be no more religions. People will simply follow spirituality. The more people get to know their real *Selves*, the less wars, fights, hate, jealousy, and all of these lower qualities there will be.

When you know your Self you will see how futile it is to hate. In fact, you cannot hate at all. You see how useless it is to feel jealousy toward another person. Know your Self, and the need to compare will vanish fully.

This teaching is not based on philosophy or logic or argumentation. It is purely based on "Self discovery." Philosophy gives you logic. It tells you that God exists. At the same time, another person can argue about it, giving another logic that God does not exist. If I give you one kind of logic, another person's logic will be contradictory. So philosophy is based on all those arguments and on logic. That is why there is no end of books written on philosophy. How many books are written on science or on art?

You can count them. But on philosophy they are uncountable. They are countless. If you visit India and you try to compile all the books written on philosophy on a disk, you will not be able to. There are too many. You can draw infinite questions out of just one of my lectures. Why? Because as soon as I state something, you start comparing it with similar statements heard somewhere else.

So always remember that logic and argument cannot serve your purpose. They cannot give you the answer to why you are here. Logic and arguments do not belong to your soul. Actually, philosophy is the itching of the mind. And by scratching, you give your mind some relief. I don't condemn philosophy. It can be helpful at the beginning of your journey. By reading you can get some ideas, some direction. But philosophy alone cannot lead you on the right track. It cannot show you the way, especially when it says this is the only way. On this Earth there are six billion human beings. They all have different brains and different minds, so how can there be only one way?

Philosophy too, like religion, has done a lot of damage. Actually we don't need philosophy. We need to experience our being so we can know for ourselves what is the path. A dead book cannot show you the way. The path has to be shown by a Self-realized person who is present right here. Books are dead; who cares about dead books? Only if you are a novice can books help. But if you are fortunate to have an alive teacher guiding you, that will be much better. There is no need to believe my words either; experience is enough in itself. Experience helps you to realize and find the way. If you have the experience, there is no longer a need to believe. You have been taught to believe by your parents, by priests, by the fundamentalists and by religious people. All of them taught you to believe.

But have they taught you to know your real purpose? To know why you are really here? Godhood must be tasted and it can only be tasted individually, not collectively. Once you get the experience, you know that Godhood is hidden inside you. Then the need to believe or disbelieve disappears.

Gaining the courage to go through the experience breaks down all beliefs. Today you might believe that this philosophy is good or this religion is the right one. Tomorrow, as soon as you know more about its inner politics, your beliefs will change and you will start searching for something else. So why believe? Philosophies and religion teach beliefs. I don't teach belief at all.

Philosophy and religion are the biggest manipulations on Earth. Let me tell you why. By following any philosophy or any religion, you don't have to work on yourself. There is no need to awaken your inner guru. That's why. Your Self, your inner guru, once awakened, is the only true teacher you will ever need. But you are asleep – your inner guru is asleep. That is why, at first, you need the help of an outside guru. The outside guru shakes you so that your inner guru can be awakened. So if you ask me what spirituality does for you, I will tell you that it enables you to find the process of how to awaken your inner guru.

You can learn from everything. You can learn from philosophy and from religion, but make sure you do not get stuck there. Make learning your spiritual pursuit. You have to enlighten yourself - otherwise you will miss the truth. Your purpose is to flower fully, to shine without any purpose like the sun, like the stars or the moon. Allow whatever happens along the way to happen without any purpose. Simply flow and one day you will arrive there.

In this life, the most important thing to learn is to learn to know your Self. Just be. Remember: you have infinite power. You are not a body, you are not a mind, and you are not thoughts. Everything that happens along the way is helping you to know your Self.

You are very lucky to have a well-developed mind. Other earthly creatures are not as lucky as you. Animals might have instinctive power, but you have a developed mind. A developed mind helps you to grasp the teaching. If in this life you are fortunate enough to meet a teacher, or a Guru, don't miss the opportunity to learn from such a person. A developed mind has the capacity to receive what the alive teacher is trying to convey through your being, and once your being is filled with light, you will be always in bliss. In this state your body and your thoughts will be totally relaxed. You will not believe it is happening to you. For the very first time you will be able to experience your Self. When this happens, your life will have taken a one hundred and eighty degree turn.

I am telling you that if in this existence you can experience your being or meet your Self, you will be the most blissful person. However, to meet your *Self* you have to stop clinging to religion and philosophy. Clinging to them and going from place to place. One day you will realize that all clinging is a vain effort and that whatever you were searching for was always with you. Clinging to anything is false. First you must understand the direction, then you will have the courage to walk the path on your own.

Any direction is like a finger pointing to the moon. The finger is the direction, while the moon is your Self - your *real* Self. You have to search yourself. Your being is hidden inside of you, and one day, if you try, you will find it. It is like the butter still hidden in the milk. Can you get the butter out of the milk without knowing the process? No, you cannot. You cannot simply sit and stare and pray for the milk to turn into butter, can you? It is the same with your being. Your being is hidden in your body underneath your mind. Mind means thousands of borrowed layers with your being buried underneath all of them. But how did this happen? It is simple. One layer is given to you by your parents: peel it off. Your friends give another layer to you: take it out. Another layer is given to you by society: again, peel it off. Certain schools give layers of ignorance, so peel them off. The more layers you remove from your mind, the lighter you will become. Do you know what you will find in the end? Assume that you are peeling an onion. After peeling it layer by layer, what is really left at the end? Nothing. It is the same with you. After peeling all the layers from your mind, what is left is nothing, and that nothingness is the *real you*.

Don't consider your body to be one of the layers. This body is your house; it is the temple in which you reside. You must be thankful to your parents, no matter in which circumstance you were born. Right now you are here and you have the possibility to realize and find your real Self. Be thankful to your parents for giving you the opportunity to be here. Because of them, you can discover yourself fully. Remove all the layers from your consciousness. You can discover the truth of your nakedness right now. Truth has no layers – you cannot feel it. The more naked you become, the closer to inner silence you will get.

I am here sitting on this chair with you, writing and telling you so many things, telling you to realize your true Self. I am walking with you, I am living with you, I eat what you eat and I drink what you drink. I don't resist at all. Is this where you want to go? Then work on your emotions. Work on your anger and be relaxed. If you learn this then one day you too can convey to others what I am conveying to you. No matter what situation you are in, no matter if it is a good or a bad situation, you must learn not to be affected by it. You have abilities, you have infinite power, and if I have reached and tasted this relaxed state, you can reach it too. Everybody can taste it if they work slowly, step by step. This is the reason why I teach slowly. I don't teach jumping – maybe I teach yoga jumping exercises – but I don't teach to jump on the path so you can reach your destination faster. I teach you to go slowly. Always remember that slow and steady wins the race. If you try to jump from the start – from the top to the bottom – you might fall and be seriously hurt. Don't get too excited. Be patient. Simply listen to your spiritual guide and maybe one day you will know your own path. Only your own path can lead you to find who you really are, to transform your life completely.

Your life will then be your art, and everything you do - speaking, giving lectures, writing books, writing poems, making sculptures, being an expert at the computer or typing – will indeed be an art. Your creativity will blossom and you will be filled with love. You cannot be stopped. More and more creativity will surface, and if you are a painter your art will be very rare and unusual.

I remember a Zen story. A disciple came to his master asking to teach him how to find himself. The master suggested painting a bamboo tree. The disciple, who was a true seeker, tried. He painted the most beautiful bamboo tree. He took the painting to his master but the master was not satisfied. He said to the student, "You have painted a very beautiful tree, but it is lifeless, so try to paint it again." The student tried thousands of times and he was rejected every time. The master said to him, "Don't come back to see me until you are able to paint life in this tree. Why are you sitting here with me? Go to the forest and paint."

The disciple went to the forest and sat under many bamboo trees. After some time, he began to have experiences. He felt that a certain kind of energy was coming to him. He instantly recognized it to be his only possibility, and he thought, "Maybe this was what my teacher meant."

He spent days and days painting. He even stopped eating. Eventually he began to feel oneness with the bamboo trees. After one year, maybe two, he felt a connection with each and every one of the bamboo trees in the forest and he had become almost a bamboo tree himself. In the meantime, the teacher became curious, and wondered how come two years had passed and the student still hadn't come back. One day someone told the master that he had seen this great and very intelligent student always sitting under the bamboo trees and he seemed like he was acting and reacting just like them. The teacher, after hearing this great news, could not resist seeing him. He went to the forest and he found the student with a piece of paper in his hands. The teacher took the paper from him and saw that he had drawn a bamboo tree. Satisfied with what he saw, the teacher said, "You have done well. I know now that you have experienced it completely. You know what it is to be a bamboo tree."

True art, true creativity, reflects your being everywhere because it is you. And if someone asks you to place a value on it, you cannot, because it is priceless. If you want to be an artist, experience your aliveness. It does not matter if you create one piece or hundreds of pieces of art. What matters is that that your *being* is reflected in your art. If you want to understand what true art is, understand your Self. Choose the spiritual path and discover your *being*. Learn the process of how to turn milk into butter. Experience life to its fullest. Then you will realize your true and real Self. This is what it is to be spiritual.

SPIRITUAL GROWTH

Spiritual growth is a very different kind of growth. In a way, it is not growth at all. When you have a job or you deal in any business, you see results. You get something for your effort, and receive pay for your effort, which satisfies you. But when your effort doesn't pay off, you become dissatisfied.

Spiritual growth, or growing spiritually, is very, very different. When you begin to follow and listen or to read about spirituality, you get the feeling that a big treasure awaits you at the other end. But when you really start following it, and the more you become involved in it, nothing seems to be there at all. Why? Up to that moment, all of your experiences have been strictly focused outside of yourself on the material world. However, because spiritual growth is completely different and unfamiliar to you, the only thing you see when you enter into it is darkness. It seems there is no inner treasure. But if you persist, the moment will come when the treasure is discovered.

When you first enter your inner Self, you see nothing but darkness; nothing is visible, and nothing is gained. The only thing you notice is how others see you. You become aware of their thoughts, and you know that

most people around you think you are going crazy and that you are
wasting your life. In one way, they are right.

In the beginning of the journey, when you close your eyes to go within,
you see only dark; nothing else is visible. But no one knows how powerful
this is. To experience the dark is the first step into spiritual growth. The
real treasure can only be found in the dark.

In India, our first prayer was: *Tamso ma jyotir gamaye.* "Oh, Lord, lead us
from darkness to light." In my opinion, you have to follow darkness first,
because if there is no darkness there cannot be light either. Where there is
deep dark and you light a candle, that little flame will shine very much.
Light without the dark has no meaning at all. It is the dark which gives
meaning to light. I really think that the first step into growing spiritually is
to sink into the dark. By sinking into the dark, it seems you are not
achieving anything. In actuality, this is not true. You are achieving a lot of
things. To walk in the dark is frightening. However, by following the
spiritual path, all of your fears will go away and your courage, boldness
and will power will increase. With time, you will come to understand this.
Others will see it, but not until much later.

So to grow spiritually is a very different phenomenon. To the naked eye it
seems you are not gaining anything. In fact, you seem even unhappier as
time goes on. But it is not really so. The truth is, you are getting many
things, but none of those things are visible until later. This is why spiritual
growth is very difficult to understand. But once you understand and once
you taste it, you are eager to taste it again and again and again.

You will encounter many difficulties and your mind will constantly play tricks on you. It will disturb you by trying to take you away from achieving your goal. It will trick you into thinking it is not good to go into the dark, and it will try to create unhappiness in you. Your mind, and others' opinions, will persuade you to stop. You will be constantly tempted to leave your spiritual aspiration and find happiness in the outer world. But if you think of quitting, I would strongly suggest that you not listen to either your mind or to the opinions of others. Go deep into the dark, and then you will come to know that real happiness is not an outer thing but an internal phenomenon, which can only be found by passing through the dark. Eventually, by passing through all the difficulties you encounter along the way, real happiness will be achieved. And once you achieve it, you will never lose it.

Many people seem to be very happy, but just to seem happy is not happiness. On the contrary, it means that your happiness can become unhappiness at any moment. This happiness is merely a surface experience. For example, if you unexpectedly get some money, you become very happy. But after you have spent it, your happiness is gone. This shows that your happiness was not real. The fact that you are again unhappy shows that it was not an eternal experience, but rather a motivated experience.

This is why people who do not practice spirituality seem to be even happier than the people who follow a spiritual path. But the happiness of those who don't practice spirituality is not real. Their happiness will vanish if they do not keep on sustaining it with different activities. The happiness I am talking about is quite different, though. It does not come because of doing anything; it is discovered in the state of *being*.

In the outer world, people seem happy because their minds play tricks on them. The mind plays a lot of tricks. Actually, it is like a monkey, or like a big marketplace. When you visit a market, or when you visit a mall or a store, you see there are many, many things, and you think it is wonderful. So you try to make a lot of money to get all of these things. Getting – acquiring – gives you a lot of happiness. But this happiness is there only for a while; it is not eternal. You must work or read or do more things to keep it up. Mind is never satisfied. This is why you have to constantly be doing something. But if, by your spiritual growth, happiness is achieved, such happiness will last forever.

Real happiness always comes from inside. It is an inner phenomenon, and it can come only if you have achieved right understanding. This happiness is not cause and effect; it is your pure state of being. It has nothing to do with our worldly things. If you can achieve this kind of happiness, you should rest assured that it will never leave you.

Pass through the dark and persevere until you come to the light. Allow happiness to be the result of your experience. I guarantee you that it will last forever. Actually, when it happens, this happiness is considered to be bliss. It does not come easy, and the journey is difficult. It feels as if you are climbing Mount Everest. And you know how difficult it is to climb Mount Everest! Spiritual climbing is even harder than that. So if you want real happiness – eternal happiness – you must pass through the dark. Whether you are rich or poor is irrelevant regarding the attainment of this happiness, because this happiness has nothing to do with your outer conditions. If by passing through the dark you acquire right understanding, happiness will be the result of your achievement. Actually, this happiness is who you really are.

There is a saying in India: *Santosh eva manushyanam paramum dhanam.* – "Real satisfaction is the only real treasure, and if you can attain it, only then you will be very happy." Outward things can make you happy, but that happiness is temporary. It does not last forever. Don't trust in that happiness; search for the real happiness. This is spiritual growth. This is the doorway to happiness.

MIND IS THE SERVANT

Once a king posed a question to a master and to a teacher: "How can this mind of mine, which became the master of the soul, master of the being, which is all in all, become the servant and follow me, instead of me following it?" The teacher, who was very wise, thought that to merely answer the king's question might not bring the king to a total understanding. He needed to give the king a practical example in order for him to come to know the answer. So the wise man said, "Yes, I can answer your question, but you must do one thing. Go and declare to the whole town to bring to the court a fully fed goat, and if the goat refuses to eat more, then the owner of the goat will win $1000. But if the goat eats, instead of winning the $1000, the person will have to pay a fine."

The king went ahead and made his declaration, and thousands of people came forth with their goats. Their goats had all been fed everything possible for the whole day. But when the goats were put to the test and the grass was put in front of them, they ate it. Nobody won, and each contestant had to pay the fine instead.

Then a very ordinary person appeared in the court. The man, who seemed to be very poor, came to the king and said, "I can do it and I will win too, but you have to give me one day to prepare." The king agreed. The next day he came with his goat and the goat was put to the test. The green grass was put in front of the goat, but the goat completely refused it without even looking at it. The owner was declared to be the winner. The king was amazed, and his curiosity compelled him to find out how it had happened. He wanted to know how the man had managed to train his goat to not even look at the green grass. "It was simple," the man said, "I took the goat in the field, but I did not allow him to eat any grass. As soon as I saw him looking at the grass, I hit him on the head. This went on for the whole day, and I did not let him eat anything until I was satisfied and saw that he was trained. I kept the whip in my hands and every time the goat attempted to eat any grass, I whipped him on the head."

This is the way. If you want to train your mind and have your mind follow you, you must take out your whip and hit it whenever it is needed. Mind wants everything, and in fact, of the five senses, the mind is actually considered to be the king of the senses. And the senses can never be satisfied. No matter what kind of dessert you had the day before, the next day, if you see another kind, your mouth will water again. No matter how many beautiful things you see through your eyes, when more beauty comes your way, you cannot resist it. This goes on and on for your whole life. No matter how much beauty you see or how much fragrance you smell, you will never be satisfied. Remember, I am talking only about the senses; I am not talking about the mind, which is the king of the senses. No matter how much you try to fulfill your mind's desires, your mind will never be satisfied. And what do you do? You follow your mind all the time. No wonder your mind has became your master. You choose going to the movies before you choose meditation. You choose going to a sale before you choose meditation. You choose, and this choosing strengthens the mind, leading you astray and away from yourself. But if you begin to see that *choice* takes you away from yourself, you might stop or bypass your mind. Somehow you must learn to bypass your mind. To bypass your mind means not to pay attention to it. The TV might be on, but if there is nothing interesting, you will pay no attention to it. But as soon as something interesting comes on, your attention will be captured again. To bypass the mind means to remain with one's Self at all times unless you are needed for other tasks.

Bypass your mind and you will have learned the greatest art. I assure you if you learn this art your mind will become your servant for sure. Learn this as soon as possible, because right now you are still encased within your mind. But if it is difficult for you to bypass, then the other way is to discipline your mind. Through discipline, your mind can be trained just like the poor man trained his goat not to eat the grass. By the use of the whip he trained his goat. It was not easy for him to keep on whipping the little goat, and neither will it be easy for you to keep on whipping your mind. It is up to you how you want to do it, but these are the two ways. Most people understand the language of discipline. So if discipline is what you need, then discipline yourself and your mind will follow and serve you. Otherwise, you will remain powerless and a slave to your mind. Work on it and understand what is happening, because once your mind becomes your servant, enlightenment is not far away. Enlightenment is already there anyway. You are already the bud which can blossom into a rose at any moment.

205

AWARENESS: THE KEY TO HAPPINESS

Awareness is the key to happiness. But what does it mean to be aware? To be aware means to be present, watching over everything that happens in a calm and relaxed way. When you are in your house, you are aware of many things. If something is missing, you notice it right away. If something is added or put in the wrong place, you notice it right away. Even if something needs to be done, you will be aware. Whether you do it or not is not as important as being aware.

Having this kind of awareness is considered outer awareness. On the other hand, when you begin to look inside you might become aware of yourself within. Presently, even if we are looking within, the only thing we might be aware of is our mind with all of its emotions. Again, this awareness too, and even though it seems within, is still considered outer awareness. Very rarely do we find someone who has reached into his or her depths and become aware of the soul, and to be aware of the soul is considered inner awareness.

The body is made of gross matter, while the mind is made of subtle matter. Even though mind is an inner experience, it is still considered material, and anything material is visible. You might say, "But I do not see my mind. It is not visible, therefore I do not consider it to be material as the body is." In truth, you are partially right, but only partially right. Because you have not yet begun to work on yourself to develop your inner vision, you are unaware of this fact. Develop your inner vision and you will see that the mind too is made of material substances, perhaps less apparent than the physical body, but still material.

In the outer world you are already aware of many outer things. But have you ever thought of becoming aware of who you really are? How many times have you asked yourself: Who am I? Why am I here? Why have I come here? Why do I always remain in this body? Where did I come from? Where do I go once I leave this place called Earth? These are questions that some of us have asked ourselves, and because of it, our inner journey into Self-discovery has started.

So the spiritual journey means becoming aware of the Self within. In doing so, you can discover many interesting things and can experience moments of great peace, stillness, ecstasy and great confidence.

You already have awareness of your outer self, and now you are aware that the mind is made of material substance, even though it is subtle. You are also aware that at death everything material stays here and that all of its functioning power will be gone. Scientifically, it has been proven that the body is the combination of five elements: water, air, fire, earth and space. Logically you understand that once you die, the body, which is the combination of these five elements, is still visibly present, but the empowering force is missing. That's what you need to be aware of. It is your soul you now need to work to realize.

But you are not aware of your soul. You are only aware of the material aspect of you – your mind, and the combination of the five elements, but not of the power behind them. You are merely aware of that which is not eternal and which ends in time. No material things can be considered real. All is illusion. This is why it is very important for you to acquire the right understanding of what is real, or what is truth, and what is unreal or illusion. How do you acquire right understanding of reality? Simply begin to look at things for what they really are. Take water, for example. The true nature of water is always cold and always liquid. Isn't this true? But somehow you just got burned with some hot water. Your first impulse is to think that the hot water burned you, when in reality it was the fire that burned you. The nature of water is cold, not hot. Fire heated the water. So if you begin to look at things with the right understanding, you will discover the truth. The water was hot, not because of its nature, but because of the nature of fire. That is what correct understanding means.

You need to really look and understand the true nature of things, how things really are. The same goes for you. If you identify with your body, or with your mind, or with your thinking, you are not identifying with reality. By definition, you are in illusion, and illusion does not have anything to do with reality, or with truth. Presently, you are still in illusion. You are not yet aware of your soul. It is your mind that is controlling everything. Your mind controls every action you take, including every thought you think.

Mind means duality, and mind dwells in the past or the future, never in the present. You might have a positive mind so everything you do is positive, or you might have a negative mind and everything you do turns out negative. But you are beyond any aspect of positive or negative, good or bad, right or wrong, love or hate. All this is nothing but duality, and the soul is beyond duality. The soul functions vertically. It is infinite, therefore, it is constant and aware of itself. Mind, at the other end, is itself illusion. Mind is like the horizon, which can never be reached.

You know very well that once the past is gone it is gone forever, and the future never comes. If you understand the moment, you will come to understand the vertical line, which is the soul, or God. Christians have depicted it correctly. The vertical line on the cross represents God, while the horizontal line represents the mind. What is this telling you? If you want to achieve Godhood you must surrender your human self (or that horizontal line) to the vertical line, as Jesus did, and you will be in the Kingdom of God.

So the mind is illusion – it is duality. But you can transform this duality. In fact, it is the master key to unlock your soul. You need to have a clear understanding of this because once it is understood the mind can easily be bypassed. Soul can be freed only if you can go beyond duality. If you can't do this, you will remain in illusion forever. You alone can make this choice. If you make it, you will gain the awareness you need to liberate your eternal Self. Awareness is therefore the key to awaken your soul and achieve that happiness which is beyond duality.

DYING WITH AWARENESS

It is said that Lao Tzu was born as an old person. Naturally, he was born as a baby, carrying with him all memories of his previous life. But in China it is believed that he was born as a wise man, which is why it is said he was born old.

There is a way in which one can carry all memories forward into a new life. Unfortunately, no country in the world has experimented with this process, except Tibet. A very long time ago, Tibet, now under the rule of China, was the first country to experiment with this process. This process is called Bardo. In Tibet, Bardo is a very popular concept. When an individual begins the process of dying, Buddhist monks gather around the dying person. They help the person to remain aware and they constantly send messages such as: "Now you will feel that your breath (life force) is leaving your body, your mind, and your thoughts. You will feel like the sun, high in the sky, melting the ice." Sometimes they have to shake the dying person back to awareness until the moment when life has fully left the body. In the Bardo system, if you can die this way, you will carry all of your memories into your next life. But why don't people have any memories of their previous life? Because they did not die with awareness. This is why all memories are lost.

Unfortunately this system is only practiced in two of the oldest world religions, the Buddhist and Jain religions. The Jain religion says, "If you die with awareness, even one death is enough for you to remember your previous life and all the mistakes you had made. Then you will never repeat them again." Can you imagine if you remembered your previous life? Could you repeat the same mistakes? It would be impossible.

In the Western world, only one person was aware of this system. Ouspensky, who was well known by many, was determined to experiment with dying with awareness. So he chose to die while walking. Before dying he said, "I want to carry all the memories of this life with me." So he gathered together all of his friends, all of his relatives and all of his students. He asked them to walk with him, and as he walked he was saying, "I am leaving my body, but I want to leave it while walking. I want to walk and be aware. If I lie down, it is possible I might lose all memories. You never know: I might be in a coma and forget everything. I want to carry everything with me." So he went on walking and saying to his friends, "Now I feel like I am losing my body." After a few more seconds he said, "I am losing my breath." He walked until he died. He was aware, and he was able to carry all of his memories with him. It is a difficult process, and he was the only person in the West who died with awareness. But in India and in Tibet, a surprising number of people have died with awareness.

Actually, we think this is our body, but it is not. This body is here temporarily. You might reach one hundred, even one hundred and fifty years. Still, your body is temporary.

212

This body can die at any time, and once it is gone, you get a new one. It is just like changing clothes. This body is not the real body. The real body is inside of this gross body. The real body is called the subtle body. It is the subtle body that carries all the memories, but unfortunately it is invisible, and thus it is not easily perceived. It must be activated because it is our connection between this life and future lives. The best way to work on the subtle body is to work on awareness.

It is not easy to get ahold of the subtle body and all of its subtle experiences. Imagine sitting by the bank of the river and watching its flow over a very flat surface. The water is without sound. It makes no ripples. There is total stillness. If you sit quietly and peacefully, you might hear the soundless sound of water flowing. And if you can hear this, you might develop the possibility to work on your subtle body. It takes much sensitivity to hear the soundless sound of flowing water. But it takes even more sensitivity to perceive the subtle body.

Zen, which is a spiritual practice in Japan, trains you to hear one hand clapping. It teaches you to develop sensitivity, and in developing sensitivity, you might become aware. This is why Bardo works in Tibet, and the Jain practice of *samlekhana* works in India. In the West, too, Ouspensky followed the Bardo practice, but none of his students did.

You will be surprised how many memories you can find stored in your subtle body if you begin to work on it. In one computer chip you can store billions of bits of information. But in your subtle body, your storing capacity is millions and millions of times greater than a computer chip. It can store the whole universe – millions of galaxies. You do not need to search the millions of galaxies by satellite. It is all here, all in your subtle body.

There are many ways in which a person can work on his or her subtle body. The best way is to be aware at the time of death. But luckily you don't have to wait until then. You can start right now, because once your subtle body is activated, everything around you seems transformed. Everything appears beautiful. You might recall some events in your life that were significant. You might remember the time when you fell in love, and the person seemed so beautiful to you even though in reality he or she was simply ordinary.

In love, everything appears beautiful. Ask anyone who is in love how he or she sees his or her beloved. He will tell you that she is the most beautiful lady he has ever met, or vice-versa. Why? The feeling of love creates a reaction that releases chemicals into the body giving the person feelings of euphoria. When the body is not stimulated by these chemicals, it is much more difficult to see beauty in everything. Drugs function the same way, which is why people are sometimes attracted to them. When someone takes LSD, for example, the most ugly person becomes the most beautiful person. When such chemicals are secreted, the whole universe becomes incredibly attractive. In the case of Romeo and Juliet, Juliet was ordinary, but because Romeo was so much in love, she became the most extraordinary vision to his eyes. In love, even the most ordinary person becomes the most beautiful person in existence.

Well, I never suggest that you work through LSD or merely falling in love. I suggest that you start working naturally on the subtle body. Why wait for death to work on it? Start right now. You can learn the steps with the help of an expert on the matter. Even if you only learn how to travel into your body's system by using your breath, you will still become the most incredible person. To get there it takes a lot of courage, a lot of confidence, a lot of peace, calmness and tranquility, like sitting by the bank of the river hearing the soundless sound of the water.

LIFE

When you think of life, ordinarily you think of life in society. You think that the meaning of life is to be with friends and family, to be with your children, to make a living, to make a good name for yourself and to fulfill others' expectations. But you do not understand that to think this way you limit yourself and miss the real meaning of life. Life is a much broader phenomenon.

In Sanskrit, *jivitam* is the word used to describe life, while *jivinam* is synonymous to jivitam. Jivinam and jivitam do not translate exactly as life, but as alive and aliveness, respectively. Jivinam and jivitam both describe something which has feelings and sensations. If there are no feelings, no sensations, no pain – and if happiness or sorrow are not felt – it means that life is gone and that death has occurred: that *jiva*, or soul, is no longer present.

A table, for example, has a life expectancy of "x" number of years even though the presence of jivinam or jivitam is not there and the table has no feelings, nor sensations. If the table can feel something, it means it has life; it is alive and it has jiva, or soul. It is the soul, therefore, which feels pain, happiness, unhappiness and sorrow. The soul feels everything. If the

217

soul is missing, it means that the life form you are looking at and touching is dead, and that life is gone.

Life has many definitions, but I find one to be very accurate: *Uvavog lakhno aayaa*. This refers to the *thinking process*, where you find instincts, intuition and memory functioning. When these things are present, life is also present. Dead things don't have this process in them. It is found only in things that are alive. In India, in a very ancient book, I found a verse which said, *Jale vishnu thale vishnu vishnu parvat mastake*. It means, "Life is everywhere; it is in the water, in the sky, in the earth and in space. Life is everywhere, and in this universe there is not a single spot where there is no life, even including invisible living beings."

The five measurements or the five aspects introduce another definition, which judge if something is alive or dead. One aspect is birth. In Sanskrit, *jayate* means that which takes birth or is in the process of being born. Another aspect is *vardhate*. Vardhate shows growth. If there is no growth, it means there is no life. The third and fourth are *kshiyate* and *apakshiyate*, which also mean growth in the sense of aging or shrinking. The fifth one is *mriyate*, meaning destruction and death. Whenever these signs are present it means there is life and aliveness, meaning that life is present there. Be aware not to disturb that life. You could easily be hurting it or even killing it. Sensing and feeling also symbolize life: feeling the emotions of pain, happiness, anger, joy, pride, etc. But if none of these signs are felt, it means that life is no more. You must be careful that whenever you notice these signs you don't destroy the life you see. You must be aware that in destroying any life you collect a lot of bad karma.

So start from your own life. Go deep within yourself and remove all the layers of karma. The more you recognize your own life and the more you recognize your own being, the more you will see that the same life is flowing in every living being, and you will see that life is a universal phenomenon.

In this universe there is not a single space where life is not present. In each breath you take you swallow hundreds of thousands of bacteria, which are needed to sustain the whole of life. Without bacteria you cannot survive. Respect them and recognize that they help your survival. Even the water you drink is filled with life; it is filled with bacteria which are alive. Whatever it is, hydrogen or oxygen, these gases have life, and they are alive. This means that your survival depends on living things. No matter if you swallow air or drink water or eat vegetables, you are kept alive by living particles. Life is everywhere and not a single space is without life. So in this universe you have to be aware of how to cause the least harm.

When you can inflict the least pain or do the least killing, you can survive with happiness, and you will know what it is to respect life as a whole. So learn, and try to understand why you are here. Understand what the purpose of your life is. Know that life is everywhere, and that to survive you can't escape killing. With just one breath you are killing thousands of organisms. For survival you have to eat, but eat with awareness; eat only those foods which suffer least. Remember that whenever something is alive, it has feelings and sensations. Therefore, even the food you eat will teach you how to understand life. Understand that life is everywhere and that not even a single dot in space is without life. Once this is understood, you can continue enquiring what life's real purpose is. When you can do this you will realize life's real purpose.

Have you ever asked yourself what life's real purpose is? Is it simply survival? Is it to acquire wealth and fame? Or is it to live in duality as you are right now? Life is not what you know it to be. Your happiness and unhappiness, your joy and sorrow, are not what life is: life is much more. Your real purpose is to discover and find your real Self and know who you *really are*. Are you here in this life only to feel happiness and joy? Know that if this is your purpose, you will be bound to experience their opposites, sorrow and pain, too. Or would you like to learn how to always be in ecstasy and bliss? If the latter is your goal, then you must go deep into the meaning of life. There you will discover who you really are and the real purpose of life.

If you discover your Self you will not only find bliss, but you will also concurrently realize your infinite power. Yes, if you can discover your soul you will find that your soul has infinite power. But this power is hidden under layers and layers – thousands of layers – of karma. This power is your life force, which is the same life force present in every living being. It is your real essence.

For a moment, just think of the sun. The sun spreads its power, and its power is infinite, but one day it will end. Not right now, but perhaps after millions of years. Your soul functions the same way, but with the difference that your soul will never end. Your soul has no beginning and no end; it has infinite energy and infinite power – but you have to discover it. Yes, I have to admit that Self-discovery is a struggle, and that's why sometimes life seems to be so complicated. In reality, life is not complicated – not really. Survival in society is complicated. Actually, survival is not only complicated among humans; it is a struggle as well in the kingdom of animals, insects and birds. But the more civilized a society becomes, the more the need for survival expands. Therefore, the more complicated human lives become. Man spends all of his life's energy – whether his life span is sixty, seventy, or even one hundred years – only for survival, acquiring prestige, fame, etc., but is never interested in realizing life's real purpose. The reality of your life is to destroy all the layers and layers of karma, because only after you have removed all these layers can you really see the *real Self* and know *your infinite power*. Uncover this power, your soul power; don't let it be hidden anymore.

Who is speaking right now? This body is not merely a body. It is a temple which houses the light of the soul, and it is through this light that the body functions. If this light is gone (if the soul is gone, the body will not function), the mind will not function and the brain will not function. Nothing will function. The structure will be there, but the real essence is gone. That's why it is important to discover the power behind the structure. This power is what life is. Life means soul; it does not mean survival in society. The real meaning of life is aliveness, and aliveness has its own power. It has tremendous power. It has infinite power and it is never ending. It is eternal and it never dies.

I know you have experienced happiness many times, but still you have yet to experience life. Life is more than happiness. Life is ecstasy and bliss. If you have merely experienced happiness, you know that happiness inevitably carries unhappiness with it, and this is the main reason for your constant struggle. The happiness you know creates struggle because it merely reflects your mind, and mind means duality. In this happiness, unhappiness is sure to follow. When duality is still present, struggle is bound to be present too. So realize the real meaning of life, and know that in realizing it all karma will be dissolved, and your soul energy, the *real you*, has the chance to surface.

It is hard for you to separate yourself from pain and joy, from happiness and unhappiness, and from ignorance and knowledge, simply because that's all you know and have known. What you don't know is the fact that this is merely duality, and that duality means mind. You don't yet realize that there is something else beyond duality. Reality and truth are beyond duality. The soul is beyond duality. The soul is beyond happiness and unhappiness, good and bad, right and wrong, love and hate. Beyond all this is where you will find your real Self. Paradoxically, you must go through duality fully in order to realize your soul; you must first completely taste and realize duality. If you have not tasted or realized duality fully, there is no way you can go beyond. Only until you are totally saturated with it you will be ready to let it all go.

If you have never realized what sorrow or pain are, do you think you can go beyond them? It is difficult to go beyond them. But you cannot stand experiencing any kind of pain, and this is where the paradox lies. Refusing the pain that comes with your joy, or merely indulging in your pain and joy, will only imprison you. Also, by refusing your totality you refuse the chance for bliss and ecstasy. When happiness comes, you don't want to detach yourself from it. You search for all kinds of ways to keep it going and you get trapped in it. It is this trap which prevents *Self*-discovery. Do you think that if you are always happy you know what life is? This kind of happiness only fools you. How long can this cycle last? It can maybe last for one, two, three, or four years and then, again, unhappiness comes. If one day you come to realize how stupid it is to keep this cycle going and you get fed up with it, you might realize the truth. Once you recognize that nothing you perceive is eternal, and once life becomes meaningless to you,

you might begin to search in the right direction. But if you become depressed and stop everything instead of searching in the right direction, you will have lost the greatest opportunity to understand life's true meaning.

Life is eternal, and life means soul. Life does not mean happiness. Life is beyond happiness. Once you fully discover your own Self, you will be in a constant state of ecstasy. Just think of yourself when you are happy; you don't want to escape that happiness. But if you compare it to ecstasy or bliss, your happiness is like a tiny drop of ocean water, with unhappiness ready to surface at any time. Why do you accept being satisfied with this small drop of water? Why don't you want to search further and find the whole ocean? Can you imagine what it would be like if you found the whole ocean of happiness? If you do find it, it means you have found your soul. If you discover your Self – your soul! – all the layers of karma will dissolve in the discovery, and then your light will always shine and you will be whole. You will have gone beyond the cycle of duality, and happiness will never turn into unhappiness again. You will be in a constant state of eternal bliss and eternal ecstasy.

It is this kind of ecstasy which defines life. But the only way to achieve this extreme bliss is to get rid of all the layers of karma. This is why life is not complicated for me. Society is complicated, living in society is complicated, and survival in society is complicated. But if you could dedicate some of your time to Self-discovery, your survival in society would no longer be complicated.

The sad part is that you are merely satisfied with the drop of the ocean, and you think that you are already happy; you even feel that you are in heaven. This is why you don't search further. You are satisfied with the little drop and you have no yearning to look further toward the possibility of discovering the whole ocean. However, on the other hand, if you cannot find happiness, your desire for happiness will increase more and more and it will never end. Desires never end. What can you do then? The best thing is to begin by discovering your Self by realizing your pain, your sorrow, your happiness. And if some time you are even in heaven, experience that too. Fulfill it all, realize it all, and experience it all. Try to experience everything to its extreme. Eventually you will recognize that it is all nonsense, and you will understand that none of this is who you really are.

If it is pain, observe the experience fully. If it is sorrow, watchfully experience it fully. If it is happiness, also watchfully experience it fully. I know it may seem complicated, but you cannot find bliss or ecstasy without complication. Complications are not bad; they simply instill in you the inspiration you need in order to search and discover your soul. Don't just be satisfied with heaven; go further. Bliss – ecstasy – is found beyond heaven. Start now – discover yourself and realize both sides of the coin. The pains, the joy, the sorrow, and the happiness. Realize it all. Experience these dualities to their extreme until they automatically dissolve. You will realize and understand that *this is not who I am*, and the possibility to find your Self will arise.

Don't try to drop sorrow if it is happening; it is not possible to drop it. In fact, you cannot even go beyond sorrow unless you experience it to the extreme. Experience it and let it drop all on its own. Go on living every moment, and know that you are very lucky already to have gotten this human life, because only through this human life can you experience dualities. Duality cannot be experienced in the animal's life or the angel's life. It is only through duality that the soul can be awakened, and human life is the vehicle.

Begin working on yourself and continue until all the layers of karma or ignorance have vanished. Karma is merely darkness which covers and blocks the light of your soul. The best way to remove karma is to always be balanced, and the ways to be balanced are many. You can chant, you can do yoga postures, you can silently sit with a teacher, you can dance, you can paint, and you can sing, you can even cook or sneeze. But most of all, take the right guidance, and maybe one day you can be awakened and jump into your soul. Only then will you know the real meaning of life.

LOVE IS ONLY LOVE

Once, a poet explained love in this way:

Love is love and no words can explain it. Love cannot be brought down to logic, and questions on love cannot be answered. Questions are useless. Questions and answers belong to mathematics, not to love. Love is to expand oneself, to fully blossom and to be whole. Love is only love.

Once when I was asked who God was, I said, "God is the Whole." God is not the omnipresent and omnipotent ruler who oversees and rules the whole universe as many believe He is. God is the Whole. There was a time when kings ruled over the people. People were quite simple and uneducated and the king had absolute power over them. He used his power to do justice or to punish the people. If the king became happy, he rewarded them, and if he was unhappy, he punished them. In their eyes, the king was God. Such a strong concept remained for centuries and today you can still see it engraved in people's minds. For believers, God is the absolute power. You do good, you get good results; you do bad, you get bad results. It seems that all the prayers and all bowing to God are the continuation of the same concept.

But God is the Whole and in this Wholeness everything exists. Yes, even you. You know that your body alone is the combination of many things. This galaxy is also the combination of many things. If you just look as far as your eyes can see and expand further and further, from this galaxy to the next galaxy and to the next, putting together all of these bodies, the result is one infinite body. This infinite body is God, of which you are already one with as one of the infinite and smallest particles of existence.

In Indian mythology, *viraat* means "the expanded one." The one who has blossomed fully and become whole like an ocean. I use the ocean as analogy in order to further explain that God is nothing less than the Whole. The ocean is the combination of countless drops, while each drop is one of its parts. The ocean is the Whole and the drops are the countless and the separate parts of the Whole. Remove all drops, and the ocean will disappear. Combine all drops, and the ocean will reappear. The ocean can be lost, the ocean can be dissolved, and the ocean can be rebuilt again.

The same goes with the sun. If you see one sun, know there are countless suns and countless galaxies. Just imagine that we haven't even come close to unfolding this one galaxy, this one solar system. Can you believe that God is this infinity, and that we exist as the smallest particle of this infinity? Become viraat, "the expanded one." Expand yourself so extremely that there is no difference between you and the Supreme. You can become Supreme, but you have to expand.

I am not talking about a physical expansion. It is about your light, your soul, and your being. Through your light, through your soul, through your being, you can reach millions of galaxies. Even right now you are here, but your eyes can reach millions of miles away. You have the ability to be whole. Actually, you are already whole. You just need to realize it. Don't limit yourself any more by accepting being such a little thing, devoid of any creative ability. For example, can you separate a dancer from the dance? No! Even though two words are used, the dancer and dance are one thing. The same goes when it comes to the Self and the Supreme. Self and Supreme are one in the same. We need to be awakened. We must blossom like a flower. When the flower is fully blossomed, nothing is left to expand. The flower has become whole. It is we who choose not to become whole.

Human nature is the complete opposite of nature itself. A big tree and a little plant can grow side by side without any competition. But a poor man next to a rich man cannot stand or accept each other. They will compare. The poor man will even blame God for being so unfortunate. You have the ability to expand. Actually, not only do you have this ability, but every living being has it too. Light is light in a human, in an animal, in an insect and in every living being. The whole of existence has the same ability. Why don't we blossom, then? We cannot blossom because we block the way by our lack of effort.

We do many things, but we have never attempted to put our effort in the right direction. Our effort is put into all kinds of things but in realizing we are already a part of the Whole. We don't have any interest to know and realize who we really are. Is our purpose merely to be born and die? You know very well that human life doesn't last forever, even if it lasts up to one hundred years. When the end comes, one hundred years feels like nothing. I was asked once how long I have been following the spiritual life. I was astonished to see that thirty years had passed so rapidly. Life goes fast and we are not aware that we are missing its real purpose. Why can't we make the best of it? Expand: become viraat.

Viraat is the real meaning of love. Love means to expand, to spread, and to blossom until you are fully flowered. Love has nothing to do with what people think. Love as people know it is an emotion. But love is emotionless. When love is mixed with emotion, you have already limited yourself. But if you use emotion as a vehicle to understand love, your blossoming is certain and you will become viraat. Expand your love and be new in every moment.

People fear going beyond emotions. They think that to go beyond emotions is to be dead. On the contrary, you will always be in ecstasy, but you must be free of expectations. Love unconditionally, just like a mother's love for her child. A mother's love is unconditional and free of expectations. But in order for her love to blossom, her love should not be limited to only her children. Her love must expand to the whole of existence, or love is blocked.

Can you expand your love toward every living being? Can you expand your love towards the whole of nature? I think we all have the ability to expand our love. There is no difference between the Supreme and us. We are all the same and we are always connected. If you can understand this concept, you can definitively expand yourself, and once you expand you become God, you become viraat. You are light, and light is in every living thing. Just close your eyes and you might see millions of stars and so much more. Once you start expanding, once you start blossoming, and once you start flowering, all of life's mysteries will unfold. You don't need your senses then. Your *soul* is enough to see everything, everyone and everywhere. You will be always in ecstasy. Maybe you don't have a house or riches, but you will be in ecstasy. Poor or rich, whoever understands this concept can be in ecstasy.

There is no need to go to the mountains to meditate as in old times. Simply sitting in your home, you can travel to distant galaxies. Indian mythology tells that their prophets such as Mahavira and Buddha got fed up with all their riches and abandoned their palaces to go to the jungle. Nowadays it is not necessary to take such a drastic turn. It is not needed to leave everything behind in order to be Self-realized. You can remain at home and learn from there.

Actually, it is easier to get fed up with wealth than with poverty. Lord Mahavira, who was born in the royal family, really got fed up and he left everything behind and did the opposite. Buddha was also born in a royal family, with all kinds of privileges. He too soon got fed up with wealth. Yes, one can be fed up with too much wealth. But with poverty, one doesn't get fed up as easily. Try to help a homeless person by offering him a job and you will see that after a couple of months he will be back to the street again. His habit to survive on the street is stronger than your help. He goes on begging rather than working for his money.

When people get fed up with being rich they might search for the right direction, and if they are lucky they might meet the right guidance; otherwise they will get lost even more. This is my opinion: when the student is ready, the teacher appears somehow. It is a blessing to be rich. It is a blessing to be intelligent. But it can be a curse too in many ways. Suppose that when a person becomes a doctor or a scientist such accomplishments and intellectual achievements steer him or her into thinking he or she knows it all and then they get lost into it.

People don't try to explore beyond the knowledge they have gained. Their intelligence becomes a curse because they get lost in it. They are highly educated, but they cannot learn beyond blood vessels and bones, or beyond discovering a new cure. Actually, their ego becomes the preventing force. At the other end, however, a very simple person can be suddenly enlightened. Kabira, an Indian poet, once recited this line: "I never touched a pen or ink." He did not know how to read or write, but his poetry was marvelous. In India, the day begins with Kabira poetry broadcast on the radio. He was never educated. He was very simple and yet somehow he achieved that state of consciousness where everything flows easily. Scientists have the ability to go in that direction, but they block themselves fully.

Intellectual people have a lot of abilities, but their own intellect blocks them. I have seen judges who on the chair give justice or injustice to people and say, "In my dictionary, there is no such word as impossible." But if one of their children gets sick with some incurable disease, be sure that these same judges will run to the church and will break down to pray. Still, at the same time, they say there is no God.

If you completely break down when something drastic happens to you, it means you haven't fully grown up. You need to make yourself steady and strong, as strong as you can be. But this strength can only come if you start searching in the right direction. If you are realized, you are flowered, you are blossomed, you are expanded, you are at a higher state of consciousness and the entire equation will be solved on its own. This is why I started with "love is love." There are no questions when it comes to love. There is no why; why cannot be answered. Love means to expand.

Love means to be whole. If you can start, start today. Feel the love you feel toward your child toward a bird, toward a dog, toward a plant, toward the ocean, the rivers and the stars. If you can feel, it means you are moving in the right direction and you are expanding yourself.

Work to realize that you are part of the whole and you will know that there is no difference between you and the millions of galaxies. This is how you blossom and expand. Once you are expanded, all misery and suffering will leave you automatically. Misery and suffering do not like an awakened person.

I was in Punjab visiting this great acharya who had cancer. My teacher asked him to explain in his words how his body felt. He answered, "I am in pain the whole twenty-four hours and I feel as if my whole body is being poked with needles." He was amazing; even in such a condition he always had a smile on his face and he endured his pain with grace, even when surgery was performed on him without anesthesia. His anesthesia was to enter into a deep state of meditation.

Misery and suffering leave you once you are fully awake. Maybe physically you still experience pain, but spiritually there is no pain when you are awakened.

Expand fully and be viraat. Know that love has no logical explanation and that it is not an emotion. Increase your love to embrace the whole of existence and all misery and suffering have no other choice but to leave you. Expand and your light, your soul, and your being will be awakened. God is the Whole and the whole is viraat, "the expanded one," "the Love."

WINNING THE INNER BATTLE

People think that winning a war makes a person victorious.

There are two kinds of war: the inner war and the outer war. When a country fights another country, when a person fights another person, when a mother-in-law fights her daughter-in-law, when a daughter fights her mother, when a son fights his father, or a husband fights his wife – these wars are considered outer wars, and outer wars do not help humanity to improve. These kinds of wars only pull the soul further down into the cycle of life and death.

The real war is to fight the inner enemies. Only a few people can really fight the inner war. But those who even attempt the inner fight can become a Mahavira, a Buddha, a Krishna or a Christ.

The inner enemies are many. They are the real enemies and they must be confronted. But, if I categorize them, I will say the most powerful enemies to human evolvement are *raga* and *dvesha*. These two enemies are very powerful. They will block one from expanding consciousness or from achieving enlightenment. Raga (attachment) and dvesha (hatred) are two of the most powerful seeds to increase the cycle of life and death.

235

Attachment is our greatest enemy. We are attached to everything and we don't even realize it. But when something slips from our hands, we begin to cry, we become unhappy, and the pain we feel makes our lives miserable. Raga (attachment) is a big concept.

Hatred, on the other hand, makes us dislike many things. We might dislike a person's attitude, or the person's nature. It does not matter what it is. Whatever we don't like falls under the category of hatred.

Raga and dvesha are our greatest enemies. If we can dissolve them, we will be victorious.

There is not a big difference between you and Jesus, between you and Mahavira, or between you and Buddha. They have fully faced their inner enemies and we have not. Not to face the inner enemies blocks us from experiencing our being.

You are not far from God. God is hidden inside you. But to experience it, you have to fight your inner enemies. As I mentioned earlier, raga and dvesha are our greatest enemies and in them every emotion such as anger, ego, deceit, greediness, etc. are included. I cannot stress enough how important it is for you to work on your inner enemies. Furthermore, know that all emotions block your path to God. I suggest you never try to control your emotions. The more you try to control your emotions, the more you will block your spiritual path.

You have been taught to control your anger. I am telling you that you can never win over anger by controlling it. Anger is impossible to control.

You have heard of the *Mahabharta*. A teacher was teaching five *pandavas* and their cousins. They were five small children and five brothers. The first lesson was: "Don't be angry." The children only needed to memorize this lesson so that the teacher could test them the following day. They wrote the words and then went home. The next day, the teacher tested everyone individually. All were able to repeat "Don't be angry" but Yudhishthar. Even though Yudhishthar was the most intelligent one, he was having the hardest time repeating it. The teacher did not understand why Yudhishthar couldn't memorize such simple words. "I thought you were the most intelligent one," the teacher said to Yudhishthar. "Why can't you memorize this?" Yudhishthar replied by saying, "I was not ready for it." The teacher felt very disappointed and said, "Because of you, I cannot teach further now. You must memorize your lesson or I will have to punish you."

The teacher gave him more time. Still he couldn't memorize those three words. Out of exasperation, the teacher hit him with a stick; he hit him with his hands also, but to no avail. Still he gave him one more day to memorize it. The teacher didn't want him to be behind all the other students. Even the next day, Yudhishthar couldn't repeat "Don't be angry." The teacher couldn't understand what was wrong with Yudhishthar. All of a sudden, the teacher, who was teaching "Don't be angry," became very angry and treated him very cruelly. Still he remained balanced. A while later, Yudhishthar spoke. "Yes, now I can memorize 'don't be angry.'" The teacher said, "Just for this it took you so long?" "I memorized it the moment you uttered those words to us, but I was testing myself to see if I could avoid being angry or not," said Yudhishthar. "You tried to hit me, you tried to beat me, and now I can say, 'Don't be angry.'" The teacher thought, "Yudhishthar is not a fake; he is a real student."

A real student always tests himself, not by controlling his or her anger, but by witnessing if he or she gets angry or not. The more you try to control those inner enemies, the more they confront you. These enemies are very strong. The analogy of the ball is very good. The harder you hit or push a ball to the ground, the higher it jumps. It's the same with anger. The more you suppress or control anger, the higher it jumps. Controlling or suppressing any emotion is not the way. The way is to understand why you are angry. Ask yourself what the root cause of your anger is. If you go in that direction, you might be able to dissolve it. To dissolve any emotion is totally different than to control it. In controlling you suppress, while in dissolving you have awareness and understanding of what is happening. Once anger is dissolved it will no longer jump up at you. Understand the cause and know the root of where anger is coming from and you will be free of it.

This is the way one deals with his or her inner enemies. Inner enemies are a real danger to us and to the world around us. This is where all outer wars originate. Learn to witness your inner enemies no matter how hard it is. I assure that you will have a much easier time to face any outer war. This is what makes you victorious.

We just need to gain awareness. There are three paths or three jewels for which you can gain awareness and achieve enlightenment: *Samyag Daarshan, Jnan, Charitrani Mokshmargah,* which translate to right understanding, right knowing and right conduct, respectively. These three jewels will lead you towards the path of moksha, towards the path of liberation and enlightenment. To gain right understanding and right

238

knowing about your emotions will free you from falling into weakness. In addition, you will know how to behave with people who have no understanding. People will still try to make you angry. But if you have understanding, you will not be affected. Gain understanding and all of your emotions will dissolve.

The world is disturbed because of emotions. The Mahabharta was not a real battle. Do you really think that in such a small city like Kurushetra, such a huge battle really happened? How could hundreds of thousands of soldiers be there more than four thousand years ago? Nowadays, Kurushetra is at least a city, but in those days it was not even a village.

Objectively speaking, the *Mahabharta* is about our inner enemies and about our emotions. Yudhishtar is one of the players who represents the inner soft corner of the Self, while Douryodhan and Dushashna and all the others are nothing more than the hidden devilish aspects of self. We can be so many things at different times. Sometimes we are happy, sometimes we are sad. Some times we can handle the whole world, while other times we are totally helpless. Sometimes we are so wonderful, and in a matter of seconds we can turn into a devil.

Divinity and devilishness are both hidden inside of us. Don't think that we are only divine. The devil is there too. No wonder Christianity is always afraid of Satan. They think that no matter where they are or where they go, Satan follows them. They are right: Satan does follow them, but Satan does not come from outside; it comes from inside us. It is hidden inside and it sneaks up on us, to attack and fight us. Even if the devil can sneak in on us, it is very difficult to look at our devilhood. We seem to be happy only if we are praised. But watch out if by chance we are criticized: fury and anger will ooze out of our pores. What do we do with it? We blame the other for causing us to react. We cannot afford to think it was our doing.

One day I was among Buddhist people giving them a lecture on Buddhism. I spoke strictly about Buddhism. Knowing well that in the gathering there were two Jains, I chose not to mention anything about Hindu deities or Jain names. I was aware of their lack of enthusiasm hearing me talk merely about Buddha. They were sitting quietly, listening and feeling uninspired. Suddenly, after mentioning Mahavira's name, I noticed they had become quite alert. What had happened? Our emotions are so much in control of us that we don't care to hear anything else other than what we want to hear. But consciousness is universal, and if we are real students we can learn from anything. We can learn from a dog, a cat, a bird, nature, the river, the ocean, and yes, we can learn from the stars too.

Don't block yourself from learning. Learn from everything. If you block yourself and if God comes to you and knocks at your door and tells you, "I am God," it is quite possible you will reject him. Your close-mindedness will not allow you to believe that God is in front of you. Such reactions tell me you are not yet ready to learn. I assure you, if you are ready to learn you will learn from everything.

I want to share with you a Jain story. It is a true incident and it is about King Dadhivahan, from the Champa Puri. His pregnant wife had a craving. She was craving the smell of flowers and wanted to ride on a white elephant with her husband through a beautiful garden. The king fulfilled her wishes. He brought the elephant and they began to ride though the garden. All the trees were in bloom and the fragrance was incredible.

Then all of a sudden the elephant went totally out of control. He grabbed the trainer with his trunk and threw him away and started running crazily.

When an elephant is out of control, it is very difficult to do anything at that time. The elephant ran into the jungle and it couldn't be stopped. The king, trying to find a way to help his wife, suggested for her to grab the branches of any big tree that came their way. When they came near a big tree, the king was able to grab a branch, but the queen missed it.

Night approached and the elephant kept on going deeper into the jungle. There was no chance for the queen to find the way back now. Finally, the elephant came across a lake. When the elephant saw the water, he stopped to drink. The queen took the opportunity to get off the elephant's back. As she came down from his back, she became aware that she had to walk all alone in the dark jungle. She was overcome by fear. Still, she decided to keep on walking. While walking she realized that being afraid could cause her to miscarry the baby. These thoughts made her very strong and she walked the whole night. In the morning she saw a monk whose curiosity caused her to tell him her story. The monk understood her need to get out of the jungle. He helped and instructed her on how to get out to where she could reach the city.

When she arrived at the outskirts of the city, she saw a nun delivering a sermon. The queen was very touched hearing the advice this nun gave. The sermon made her so aware that instead of going back to her kingdom, she asked the nun to initiate her into her order. She told the nun what had happened to her, but she did not tell her of her pregnancy in fear she would not be initiated. She was accepted and she became a nun.

As time passed, she began to show signs of her pregnancy. The nun, surprised, asked what had happened to her. The queen, no longer able to keep her secret, spilled out the whole truth to her. She said, "I could not tell you about my condition in the beginning. I feared that if I had revealed the truth you wouldn't have initiated me. But I did not lie to you about being a queen and my husband a king." The nun believed her. Her concern was with the baby once he/she was born. She had to come up with a plan. After some time, a baby boy was born. But before anyone would come to know of his birth, they decided to take him away.

The baby was taken to a nearby cemetery in hopes that he would be found by a good person. The queen put her little boy under a tree. She hid herself to see if anyone would notice him and take him to their home. The cemetery caretaker, Chandal, heard a cry and followed the sound. Surprisingly, he saw a beautiful baby boy. He became so happy. He and his wife had tried for so long to have a baby, but it had never happened. It was a miracle for him to have found this little baby. He took him to his home. His wife was so happy and accepted him as her son too. They both thanked God for giving them such a beautiful son whom they named Karkandu. Karkandu grew to be a strong young man.

One day, Karkandu and his Brahman friend crossed the path of a monk. The monk told both boys, "The one of you who can remove this bamboo tree from its roots and carry it always with him one day will be a king." Both boys tried very hard, but it was the Brahman boy who uprooted the tree. Karkandu took the bamboo from him and carried it with him all the time. Upset, the Brahman boy told the story to everyone. He wanted to be the one to become a king. Karkandu, aware of his friend's disappointment, promised him one village if he became king.

All the Brahmans in the village reacted to Karkandu's doings and together they decided to take revenge on him. The incident itself created enmity between the Chandal and Brahman. Karkandu's mother, aware of what was happening and afraid they might kill her son, decided to send him to another kingdom where some of their relatives lived. In that kingdom the king had just died. In those days, kings did not leave a successor. It was customary to put a garland on an elephant's trunk and whomever received the garland from the elephant would become king. People were repeating mantras in hopes of receiving the garland. But the elephant placed the garland around Karkandu's neck. Karkandu became the new king. Once the Brahman boy got the good news, he immediately came to remind the king of his promise. The king, unable to give his friend a village from his kingdom, sent him to the next kingdom with a letter stating his request. That letter really disturbed the other king. He didn't know with whom he was dealing. So he sent his a messenger back to this new king informing that he would be attacked. Karkandu's real mother heard about this, so she rushed to save the situation. Before the fight began, the queen, Karkandu's real mother, and the older king's wife came forward to stop the fight and said, "Do you know who you are fighting? This is your son," she said to the older king. The king recognized her and became very happy. The queen told him the whole story of how she was saved and that she became a nun. Everyone became very happy and hugged each other.

There was going to be a fight, but suddenly the atmosphere had completely changed. For a little village the king could have killed his son. This incident touched him so deeply that he renounced the whole kingdom, gave everything to his son, and became a monk.

I was pointing out how a person can suddenly become enlightened. This story was an example of how quickly enlightenment can happen. You are not far away from God. There is just a little distance between you and God. But this little distance can keep you from seeing God. Psychologically speaking, God is the closest thing to you, but the closest thing is the hardest thing to see. Can you see yourself if your eyes are staked to the mirror? You need a little distance. Your heart is so open for God, but you are too close to see Him. Distance yourself to see. You never know when something might touch you deeply.

Be a real student and test yourself. We all have to face our inner enemies. Face them straight on without hesitation. Don't be afraid. If you keep them hidden, you will also keep yourself from seeing God. Open yourself and test yourself not by controlling, but by witnessing life. These inner enemies are a real danger to oneself and to the world around us. The king saw that in a moment of unawareness he could have killed his own son. Allow yourself to be touched deeply, and your being might awaken.

GOD WITHIN YOU

You need to create special qualities inside of your being. Create the color of non-violence, the color of love. Create the color of goodness. Create good thoughts. And if you are really devoted to God, God can be created in you. You can do it.

We think that God lives somewhere away from us, high up in the sky, or beyond ourselves. No, God is with us all the time. God is hidden inside our hearts, and we possess the very quality with which we can produce God inside of us. We only need to work on ourselves by shining our being.

When a cooking pot is new it is very shiny, and you can see your own reflection in it. But if it has been overused, you must put a lot of effort into making it shine, particularly if you want to see your reflection. In India they used to use ashes to make the pot shine. Your body too is like a pot. To see God's reflection, you need to create that kind of quality inside of you so you can make your body shine. If you really put all of your effort into it there is no other choice, and God has to come to you.

We carry lot of dirt in us. We carry a lot of lower qualities inside of us. Anger is dirt, ego is dirt, greed is dirt; or if you are in illusion, illusion is dirt. If you want to shine yourself, you need to clean all of your lower qualities. I assure you that if you clean them, the real face of God will appear in front of you.

Take anger for example. I have experienced that anger can sneak up on you in a hundred ways. You get angry if a child makes a noise or if someone calls you by some bad name. Anger is only an example. Many other lower qualities, such as ego, pride, jealousy, etc. can sneak up on you just as easily. You need to be aware and start cleaning these hundreds of types of dirt.

Anger alone has layers and layers and layers. Every time something affects you, another layer is being added. The more we become affected by something, the more layers we accumulate. I was merely talking about anger. Think of the other hundreds of types of dirt. How many layers do we have?

Layers and layers and layers need to be peeled. It is like peeling all the layers of an onion. What is left after the onion is completely peeled? Is the onion still an onion? No, it is not. Nothing is left. When all the layers are gone and nothing is left, God is there. God lives in nothingness. Nothingness is very important. Nothingness is like a zero, and zero represents completeness. This universe is like a zero, with no beginning and no end. Zero is a circle and a circle is always complete.

In Sanskrit, the universe is called *Brahmanda*. "*Brahm*" means God and "*anda*" means egg. In reality, we are already complete; we just need to clean all the dirt. Once we clean all the dirt, our body becomes like a shining pot where you can see God's reflection. If you want to see God, you must clean your pot, your body. Remember: God lives in a clean place. No wonder churches, temples and synagogues are kept immaculately clean. Any place of worship symbolizes your body in its totality. This is sad, but people merely understand the gross body. They think that if you shower every day you are clean. To shower is necessary, and it is a good thing to do. Outer cleanliness might help you to go a step further into yourself and clean the real dirt.

But where is the real dirt? The real dirt is found in our minds. A dirty mind is stagnant and impure. Can you see your reflection in a dirty and stagnant pond? No! If your body and your mind are dirty, God's reflection will be impossible to see. Clean it and God's reflection will come to you, and suddenly it might even awaken you.

Once a dancer was performing a dance. There were many spectators, including the king, the queen, the prince and princess, and a monk. A classical dance was being performed. Classical dancing is a special art. You have to create that kind of atmosphere so that the dance takes over. When the dancer dances, the dancer disappears, and only the dance remains. Such dancing is mesmerizing, making it impossible to take your eyes away for even a moment. Dancing in that kind of atmosphere brings you very close to God.

Her performance was magnetic and all the people were taken by it, clapping incessantly. Unfortunately, no gift was given to the dancer. Time was flowing and no one realized that the night was almost over. Even the dancer realized she had danced the whole night. She turned to her husband and said, "I danced and danced for hours and hours, I cannot go on any longer. I must stop now." Her husband replied, *"Ma Pramadi nishatyaye –*

don't be lazy; it is the end of the night now." Those words inspired her and she started her performance all over again.

The prince, sitting there, as soon as she started dancing again, took his necklace and gave it to her. In the meantime, the princess also took her diamond necklace and showered the dancer with it. Not only that: even the monk gave her his blanket. The blanket had a special quality and it was considered precious. Even though it could only be cleaned and sanitized by putting it in the fire, fire could not burn it. The monk gave the dancer his precious blanket.

The king was astonished to see that so many presents were showered on the dancer. Once the show was completed, the king made this observation to his son: "The whole night you watched this dancer and you never gave a penny, and suddenly you gave her your very expensive necklace." The prince replied, "Father, when I heard those words 'Ma pramadi nishatyaye,' – Don't be lazy, the night is ending, it is morning already – those words changed my whole life. I had planned to grab your kingdom and kill you. I had already won the heart of all my friends and convinced the army to be on my side, but those few words, 'It is morning, don't be lazy' totally changed me. I am fifty years old already and my whole life is almost gone. I don't need to create trouble now that life is almost ending by killing someone. The necklace has no meaning for me now."

The king asked his daughter why she gave her diamonds away. "Father," the daughter replied, "I am already twenty-eight years old and you haven't yet arranged my marriage, so I found a man and I arranged to run away with him and marry him. But once I heard those words 'Why are you lazy in the morning, the whole night is gone,' I reflected on my decision and I thought, 'Why do I even bother to marry? Life could end at any moment. Life has no time; nobody knows when death will knock at our door.' I thought it was not good for me to run away and bring shame to my father's name. Who knows - maybe the man just wants me for my money. This is why I gave all of my jewelry away. Jewels have no meaning for me any longer." When the person is awakened, the value of things is gone.

The king appreciated his daughter's gesture. But he was curious why the monk gave such an expensive blanket to the dancer. So he asked him, "Why did you do that?" The monk too gave the king an explanation. He said, "I have been a monk for ten years. When I first was initiated I was very happy to be a monk, but as time passed I began to doubt my vocation. I began to wonder if I had made the right decision. I could not find anything, or the so-called God. People talk about peace, but I did not find any peace or any God. I felt I had wasted ten years of my life. I was even planning to leave the monkhood tomorrow and start a new life. But the words I heard this morning created a miracle in me. I began to think I had already given ten years of my life to my calling, so why not put in a little more effort? Those words truly changed my mind. I've carried this blanket since the beginning of my monastic life and now it has no value for me any more. Listening to the words 'It is dawn, it is day light, don't be lazy in the morning', freed me to continue my path. This is why I gave my most cherished possession to the dancer."

When the right time comes and once you are inspired by even a few words, you might be awakened and be a totally different person. Be practical and start cleaning yourself. Whatever lower qualities you carry, whether it is ego, pride, jealousy or whatever, it is great if you realize they are valueless.

To clean the outside of one's self is very important, but to clean yourself from your lower qualities is much more important. This body is like a big house, and once you clean it you will be surprised: the image of God will appear right there in you. Wherever you went to seek God, you can now see it was always there in you. You just need to peel away all of the layers. God is there, awakened in you. Sometimes just a word can awaken you. Be thankful you have this life. Put forth all of your effort so you can realize God is in you right now.

ABOUT THE AUTHOR

Acharya Shree Yogeesh is a living enlightened master of this era and is the founder of the Siddhayatan Tirth and Spiritual Retreat, a unique 155 acre spiritual pilgrimage site and meditation park in North America providing the perfect atmosphere for spiritual learning, community, and soul awakening to help truth seekers advance spiritually. Acharya Shree is also the founder of the Yogeesh Ashram near Los Angeles, California, Yogeesh Ashram International in New Delhi, India, and the Acharya Yogeesh Primary & Higher Secondary children's school in Haryana, India.

As an inspiring revolutionary spiritual leader and in-demand speaker worldwide, for over forty years Acharya Shree has dedicated his life to helping guide hundreds of thousands of people on their spiritual journeys of self-improvement and self-realization. Recently, he was publicly given the highest honor in Agra, India for his spiritual work worldwide, an honor that has never been given by all four Jain sanghs throughout history until now.

It is Acharya Shree's mission to spread the message of nonviolence, vegetarianism, oneness, and total transformation.

Meet him at Siddhayatan.org and FaceBook.com/AcharyaShreeYogeesh.

CONNECT WITH US

Siddhayatan Spiritual Retreat Center

http://siddhayatan.org

Acharya Shree Yogeesh's YouTube Channels

http://youtube.com/yogeeshashram

http://youtube.com/siddhayatan

Acharya Shree Yogeesh's Facebook Fan Page

http://facebook.com/AcharyaShreeYogeesh

Contact Us

Siddhayatan Tirth

9985 E. Hwy 56

Windom, Texas 75492

info@siddhayatan.org

Books by Acharya Shree Yogeesh

Secrets of Enlightenment, Vol. I

Secrets of Enlightenment, Vol. II

Awaken!

Order additional books and audio courses online at http://siddhayatan.org

ACKNOWLEDGMENTS

Special thanks to Daniela Romero for helping create the first edition of *Secrets of Enlightenment, Vol. I*, by transcribing, summarizing and editing my lectures.

David Humphries, thank you for your assistance in editing and preparing the first edition for print.

Thanks to -
Sadhvi Siddhali Shree, for bringing this book back to life by publishing the second edition and writing the introduction. Your soul continues to shine in its creativity and deep desire to spread my teachings to all truth seekers.

Rob Secades, for the book design.
Miles O'Sullivan, for your assistance in reviewing the second edition.
Alannah Avelin, for the cover and bio photo.

But who takes care of you?
Yes, he caught the fly and brought
it outside. It doesn't belong here;
it came in by accident

Where were you born? Every where.

יְוּ דָא Juda
יִדָא Kuda

CPSIA information can be obtained at www.ICGtesting.com
Printed in the USA
LVOW13s0521150713

342766LV00004B/13/P